RATTLED AWAKE:

Volume Seven

Rattled Awake Authors

Lonnee Rey

Copyright © 2024 Lonnee Rey

All rights reserved

No part of this book may be reproduced, or stored in a retrieval system, or transmitted in any form or by any means, electronic, mechanical, photocopying, recording, or otherwise, without express written permission of the publisher.

CONTENTS

Title Page
Copyright
Introduction
Patrick Laine, PhD: "Who Are You Truly?"   1
Elizabeth Foster: "Embracing the Messy Middle: Guiding Light Through Life's Darkest Moments!"   10
Greg Spiller: "What Happened to My Internet?"   30
James McConchie: "Finding Balance"   46
Alan Chapman: "Peace Is Now"   58
Lonnee Rey: "Are You a Seeker or a Beaker?"   80
The Rattled Tattler News   95
An Open Invitation   98
Rattled Awake: Volume One   101

INTRODUCTION

We have all been through a lot over the past five years. Each of us have had multiple "Rattled Awake" moments: small and large events causing us to adjust, pivot and renew our approach to life.

These authors have shared their AHAs and epiphanies, personal revelations and advice on how they became better, not bitter, as a result.

Although their stories are wildly different from one another, in this edition in particular, there is a similar undercurrent...a theme which unifies the content unlike any other Rattled Awake volume.

Taking back authority over one's life, seeing things more clearly than ever before, discovering both truth, and one's true self - these authors bring you vital information that you can immediately benefit from, apply in your life today, and create a better tomorrow, starting right now...

PATRICK LAINE, PHD: "WHO ARE YOU TRULY?"

There's a paradox in society that the American Psychological Association has identified and studied extensively. The overwhelming majority of conversations consist of "small talk," *i.e.,* weather, TV shows, movies, etc. Yet, most people want to have deep, meaningful conversations. This paradox exists because of our desire for safety. People assume that others are disinterested in hearing something meaningful or important about themselves in conversation. However, the opposite is true as humans have a deep desire for connection and once they feel safe; tend to reciprocate in conversation. In short, if something meaningful and important is shared in conversation by one person, the other person is likely to open and share something meaningful and important in exchange, leaving both parties more fulfilled.

Today, more than ever, our fast-paced lives are full of distractions that prevent the very connection we desire most. Fortunately, there's a way to slow down and get connected with ourselves which is the precursor to connecting with others. The limitation on the depth and quality of our relationships is the quality and depth of our connection to self.

Fortunately, your subconscious mind knows you better than you know yourself. By accessing more of your nonconscious mind – the place from which 90% of your decisions are made each waking moment, you can connect with yourself and in turn, create the relationships you want. So, how do we tap into unconsciousness? Through dreams. In your dreams, you can't rely on what you see, touch, taste, hear and smell; nor can you rely on the conditions that guide your waking hours. Every scene or image in a dream is produced by your unconscious mind to serve you in some way. Sometimes, these dreams may seem "wild" or "crazy," but that's only because dream reality doesn't operate under the same construct as waking reality.

For example, let's say you want to go swimming. In waking life, at a minimum you'd take your shoes off along with the rest of your clothes before jumping in. In dream life, you'd simply jump in. We can defy gravity in dreams (flying is one of the most common acts experienced in dreams – you've likely experienced this yourself.) The first step to optimizing our ability to understand the meaning of dreams is to accept the vastly different "conditions" and rules of engagement compared with waking reality.

We have these experiences in dreams that seem so real – because they are real. The emotions we feel are real, the vivid images we see are real. Once we accept that dreams aren't fake, but simply a different reality, we can begin to open to the intended messages behind them.

Of course, for some, remembering dreams is a challenge. We don't have our senses, and that's one of the reasons why we forget dreams so quickly when we wake up, because as soon as we wake, we have an association with where we are. We know we're in our bedroom. We see the walls; we see the pictures on the wall. We see whatever we know about what happened in the bedroom. Maybe there was a fight with our spouse, or maybe an argument, etc. Something happened in that room, and subconsciously we associate it with the things that happened in our environment.

In short, location has energy. For proof, close your eyes and take two very slow deep breaths. Now imagine you're at your parents house or another place where you have a specific memory. Now, recognize what you feel. That shift in feeling is a product of the energy associated with that location.

We don't know why dreams come to us in such strange ways sometimes, but it's when we distill them and make associations with all the images. Every image that comes to us in a dream is a component of us. Relying on dream dictionaries or AI to help with dream interpretation is sufficient for entertainment purposes, but for real impact and understanding, those tools will always leave you unfulfilled.

If we look at the micro details of a dream, *e.g.*, in one of my recent dreams, there was an old lady fishing in the street with the hook sitting in midair in the middle of the street. That makes no sense right? It's silly. But as I was able to distill the details of the dream, I was able to extract the meaning and what was going on in my life at the time, and most importantly, the corrective action I could take to avoid being "hooked" (in the dream, she hooked me as I was riding down the street.) I learn about my fears. Every dream is an opportunity to learn the essence of who we are. If the whole purpose in life is to find ourselves, there's no better way than with dreams. There's no better tool, because there's no being on the planet who knows us better than our nonconscious knows us.

Fortunately, dream recall has been extensively studied and can be learned with a few easy techniques. The easiest way to start remembering dreams is to pay attention to them. Setting an intention to remember them each night helps, but even simpler, try listening to other people's dreams, asking friends and family members if they had any dreams. If you have kids, ask your kids about their dreams. The more you talk about dreams and pay attention to dreams, even just reading about dreams, the more your brain will open to it.

Speaking of kids, you think your kid is amazing. You see it so clearly, but they don't. Their low self-esteem hurts your heart. The simplest way to help them with their self-esteem is to listen to them. Ask them open-ended questions and listen. More specifically, ask them about their dream last night. Maybe they say they didn't have one. But, rest assured, if you ask that question daily for a month, they'll have one, and when they do, they'll be so excited to tell YOU because you asked. And when you listen, your relationship with them will deepen. Their self-esteem will increase, and both of your lives will change.

That is a small example of what dreams can do for your life.

To be clear, there was a time in my life when I identified as a person who didn't remember my dreams. What changed? I surely wasn't aware of the tips and tricks noted above. On February 24, 2021, my best friend passed away. The loss of such a close friend forced me to slow down and question my own existence. I suppose the term "rattled awake" is as fitting as any. Even today, three years later, I have moments where I want to call him and share my excitement about an idea or other happenings in my life.

Another "rattled awake" experience for me ties directly back into dreams. I had this recurring dream as a kid in 1986, 87, 88, (I slept in a bunk bed – top bunk right by a window.) In the recurring dream I would fly away on this magic carpet, and I would go to this pristine place - wide open space. It was beautiful. They had big giant round, very clean, boulders. I thought it was a room, but the ceiling of that place was the sky, so there was no real ceiling. It was this amazing piece of nature, and it just felt like home.

Funny enough, my love for nature today is deep. I have an abundance of fruit trees at home: four banana, mango, starfruit, avocado, longan, guava, tamarind, sapote, canistel and fig. I didn't recognize the connection between my love for nature today and my experience and feeling with that dream until this very moment, as I write today.

Now, back to that recurring dream; the dream was not something I really talked about or thought about at all from 1989 to 2022. In 2022, after 15 years married, divorced (another "rattled awake" moment) and, towards the end of 2022, I tried yoga for the first time in my life. In that moment I was overwhelmed with the realization that the mat WAS the magic carpet ("rattled awake" moment for sure.) The fact that I was able to connect something that happened in a dream, from 35 years prior, to something that happened in real life, was mind blowing.

Maybe there's a dream you remember from your childhood. Surely, I'm not alone on this one. This indescribable connection between dream world and real world, with a 35-year gap in between is what started my journey to fulfilling a purpose far greater than myself.

In early 2023 (shortly after the yoga mat realization), a friend asked "What would you say is your purpose in life?"

The question took me by surprise. After a pause, I knew the answer – "I have no purpose in life and for the first time in my life, I'm comfortable admitting it." That was the truth. We spend a lifetime chasing what we think we need to be doing; I was no exception. At that moment, I recognized the chase had ended. I could just be and just allow what was meant for me to find me. All you must do is stay in alignment and true to yourself.

This is an important point, because people need to know it's ok to just be – it's ok to not have a purpose. We constantly hear about "missions" and "purposes;" it can be overwhelming and drive us to feel less than because our timeline is different. You may have a mission or a purpose, but you may not know it at this moment, which is far better than pretending to know it.

I suppose it's no coincidence that I prioritized another purpose amid all this awakening: my role as a dad. For so long, I beat myself up for not giving my kids the childhood I had. I'll never forget another "rattled awake" moment – standing in my boat (onshore – in driveway) cleaning it out in preparation for selling it. I bought the boat because I grew up fishing with my grandfather, and I wanted my kids to experience the same pure joy. The truth was, they didn't care much for the boat – they just wanted me. All I had to do was give them their own childhood, their own set of experiences.

For those of us with fond memories from childhood, we want to give our kids the childhood that we had (or better.)

For those of us with a disappointing childhood, we want to ensure our kids have it differently (better.) My parents are still very happily married today (49 years) and I'm close with my brothers. I grew up thinking the family dynamic I had was normal. As I grew older, I realized that was far from reality for most. As magical as it was, I couldn't give my kids that life. I had to give them their life. For the first time in their lives, I became okay with that.

The result? My relationship with my kids has improved beyond what I ever could have imagined. It was only possible because I found my true self. It's our only purpose in life. Find oneself and the rest unfolds as it is intended to – FOR you. Want happiness? Find yourself.

We are each born in alignment with our true selves, but we get conditioned. As we grow up, we learn what's acceptable, what's not acceptable. We try to express ourselves. Sometimes, that expression is considered impolite or inappropriate or obnoxious. But we get slapped on the wrist and we learn what is needed to conform. We spend our childhoods trying to fit into a box. Otherwise, we'll get made fun of.

What did you hide? For me, I went to 7th grade wearing makeup on my hands, knees, and elbows to cover up my vitiligo. I wore hearing aids that I tried to hide. I didn't fit in, desperate as I was to fit in. I spent years as a kid, trying to be like the others. Perhaps that's why today, I'm so comfortable not being like others. Seriously, what did you hide?

Finding yourself is the first step – expressing yourself is an entirely different, more profound experience. The entire process is humbling – love is humble and humble is love.

Even murderers, rapists, terrorists, *etc,* they are all born good. You are born in alignment with who you are. You are also born into a circumstance that allows you to get conditioned to follow certain rules. Understanding these concepts allows us to have compassion.

You could say life is a process of peeling away the stuff that isn't us, the conditions that weren't in alignment.

I'll leave you with my favorite quote of all time (Carl Jung): The privilege of a lifetime is to become who you truly are.

Who are you (truly)?

Patrick Laine is on a mission to expand consciousness. What does that mean? The objective is to inspire connection to self because we cannot connect with others any deeper than we can connect with ourselves. Patrick is a PhD scientist with a passion for dreams. Moved by his own powerful experience with dreams – as a kid (~age 8-10) he had a recurring dream of flying on a magic carpet to this pristine place that felt like home. It wasn't until 35 years later that he stepped on a yoga mat for the first time and was overwhelmed with the realization that the yoga mat was the magic carpet. From that day forward, knowing he couldn't be the only one, his journey to discover the power of dreams and the impact they could have on our waking lives was underway. Then a year later, the vision for the world's first comprehensive platform dedicated to dreams (nighttime, daytime, psychedelic) was born. Once we connect with self, we can connect with others and build the relationships that most serve us. The journey to finding himself has led to intense fulfilling relationships with his two kids and with his life partner.

You can find Patrick on LinkedIn or dreaming with friends on Dreamigos available in the app store later in 2024.

www.linkedin.com/in/patrickdreams

Email: Patrick@dreamigos.com

ELIZABETH FOSTER: "EMBRACING THE MESSY MIDDLE: GUIDING LIGHT THROUGH LIFE'S DARKEST MOMENTS!"

The beat down was the moment I woke up, it wasn't painful; it was pale in comparison to the years I held my breath to keep the peace, live the lie, and keep it all together. My expression blanching, I laid there speechless, shaking, shocked at what was happening. I didn't swing back, I just laid there taking it, one after another. In the moment, expecting my husband to come to my rescue but then remembering he was too intoxicated to save me. He couldn't even save himself.

The next morning when I lay in bed black and blue and in pain, I wasn't offered Advil or a bag of frozen peas. It was expected that I would get up, suck it up, and keep going just like every morning after a bender. This one was different however, I couldn't just silence myself. I needed to talk to him about it. When I asked him in the nicest way possible, to leave those people out of our lives, he firmly and shockingly responded, "Absolutely not."

Recognizing Red Flags in a Relationship:
1. **Lack of Remorse:** It's concerning when there's no acknowledgment or remorse for harmful actions, such as the incident the night before.

2. **Lack of Care:** When there's no support or care after a traumatic event, such as not offering to take care of you or provide comfort.

3. **Absence of Anger:** A red flag is raised when there's no indication of anger towards those who caused harm to you, showing a lack of protective instinct.

4. **Normalization of Behavior:** Insisting on continuing with daily activities as if nothing happened, despite the severity of the situation, indicates a concerning level of normalization of harmful behavior.

5. **Alcohol as a Catalyst:** Recognizing that the root cause of these issues lies in alcohol abuse is crucial. It's important to address the underlying problem to prevent further harm.

I found myself unsurprised, though still bewildered, by our familiar pattern of sweeping things under the rug, pretending all was well. Even as I bore bruises like a walking canvas, resembling a spotted leopard, it seemed inconsequential—after all, the show must go on!

At that moment, a wave of emotions engulfed me—rage, frustration, sadness—but I pushed them aside and soldiered on as planned. It wasn't the first time I had buried my emotions; it had become a routine for me. I discovered that maintaining harmony was simpler than confronting the tumultuous emotions that bubbled within me.

We had a boat trip scheduled with friends from work, and as we set sail, it was evident they were as taken aback by my presence as I was. My husband dismissed it with a laugh, attributing it to a night of too much fun. It was a flimsy excuse, and we all knew it, yet we chose to ignore the elephant in the room.

But that wasn't the end of it. Once again, my husband drowned himself in alcohol, parading around the lake with a young blonde on his shoulders, leaving me in a state of disbelief and longing for escape. The sad truth was, I wished she would take him off my hands. Witnessing this, I'm sure those around us questioned why I tolerated such behavior. Frankly, I questioned it myself.

The only respite came when he passed out at the dinner table, allowing me a moment of solace to focus on myself. His blatant disregard for my feelings was gut wrenching, leaving me speechless, humiliated, and exhausted. I knew others pitied me, sympathizing with the torment I endured, but I couldn't shake the feeling that I was complicit, allowing it to persist.

Silently suffocating, I chose to keep the peace to avoid the tumult, enduring a slow erosion of self with each passing day. It was death by a thousand paper cuts, each one chipping away at whatever remained of me. It's true that you don't realize you're holding your breath until you exhale.
There were moments, like these, that played a loop so often I wore out the tape.

"Meet me at the bar," his texts would read, offering a reprieve from his wrath. I struggled to strike a balance between appeasing him and fulfilling my duties as a mother to our children, but often, he emerged victorious. Shame weighed heavily upon me. What began as one drink after work gradually spiraled into nights spent at the bar, leaving our children to fend for themselves with a pizza order, while we stumbled home in a drunken haze. That bottle at the bar began to demand more attention than my flesh and blood.

I attempted to rationalize with myself, slipping into the role I yearned to embody, hoping it would somehow outweigh all the nonsense.

There we sat, the picture-perfect family, gathered around the table in our cozy home, indulging in good food with smiles plastered on our faces—pretending, as always, that everything was normal. Little did anyone know, moments before we sat down, we had been engaged in a fierce battle. This was the unsettling norm in our household. The moments preceding his drinking were the most harrowing, as his words sliced through the air like a sharpened blade. I lost count of how many times I heard him belittle our daughter with hurtful words. His words, "Dumbass," echoed within me, each repetition adding weight to its validity. I witnessed the harm he inflicted upon her, yet felt powerless to intervene. His influence surpassed mine, leaving me feeling helpless. I knew everytime I said something, the response would be, "I was just kidding" or my name drawn out— "Liiiizzz"— I understood it as a command to stay out of his path. So, what did I do? I retreated, feeling like a coward, weary of enduring his unjust tirades and senseless provocations.

Are you more inclined to preserve the tranquility around you or nurture the peace within you? A question I challenge you to ponder.

I owe a debt of gratitude to the woman who jolted me from my slumber. My seemingly idyllic existence, akin to a silent movie, was built upon falsehoods and deceit. It was a time when two imperfect souls each brought their own chaos, leading to a mountain of turmoil and deceit, and a yearning for something different. Despite their desire for change, they found themselves trapped in their own patterns, unable to break free.

Identifying More Red Flags in My Relationship:

1. **Deception to Conceal Truth:** Concealing truth and disregard for feelings are alarming indicators of deeper issues within the relationship.

2. **Inappropriate Attention to Another Woman:** Behaviors such as giving attention to another woman inappropriately, especially in my presence, signify a lack of respect and boundary violation.

3. **Excessive Drinking Leading to Blackouts:** The pattern of excessive drinking leading to unconsciousness is not only concerning, but dangerous, for both parties involved.

4. **Caretaking After Disrespect:** Being forced to care for a grown adult after being disrespected is a clear indication of imbalance and lack of mutual respect in the relationship.

After that tumultuous weekend, it became abundantly clear that I had reached my limit. The events unfolded shortly after my 40th birthday on August 17th, 2019, but it wasn't until January 2020, that I mustered the courage to leave.

In the months that followed, I found myself meticulously plotting my exit strategy. I knew that timing was crucial—it had to be a moment that would cause minimal disruption to others, especially with my daughter preparing for college. So, I quietly planned, ensuring that my decision wouldn't overshadow important occasions like holidays or birthdays.

But why did I find myself orchestrating my departure from my own life? The truth is, I had spent far too long prioritizing the feelings of others over my own. The burden of enduring such pain became too heavy to bear, leaving me with no choice but to finally prioritize my own well-being.

The turmoil of that realization was overwhelming because the love I held for him eclipsed the love I had for myself. Yet, deep down, I understood that I had to prioritize my own well-being, as loving him was slowly suffocating me.

It was disheartening to realize that he didn't grasp the extent of the pain he caused me. His obliviousness to his actions only compounded the issue. I reached a point where I could no longer tolerate being treated so poorly; demanded better for myself.

I realized that the only way I could ever receive genuine love was by walking away.

Leaving him was one of the most agonizing decisions I've ever had to make. But I knew that if I stayed, I would wither away—I would never become the mother I aspired to be, and the life I yearned for would remain out of reach. So, I left it all behind: the suburban home, the children, my possessions (save for what fit in a suitcase), my pride, and even my identity.

I knew deep down that I had to chart a new course and save myself. There was no turning back. That weekend marked the beginning of my journey to self-discovery; by providing me with the space to contemplate what lay ahead. Little did I realize the challenges and triumphs awaiting me.

Looking back, I'm grateful for the uncertainty of the future because it allowed me to focus on my "why." The "how" gradually fell into place, piece by piece, as I forged ahead on my path of healing and growth.

You may see me stumble, but you'll never see me fall.

In my desperate attempt to salvage what remained of my crumbling world, I lost sight of everything that truly mattered. The irony wasn't lost on me—my efforts to control the chaos only propelled me further into the abyss of despair.

My only respite came in the form of my mother and our compassionate neighbors, who took the kids under their wing, allowing us to indulge our addiction unchecked. Countless times, I stared into the mirror, unable to recognize the hollow shell of a woman staring back at me. Had I lost her, or perhaps I never truly found her to begin with? I convinced myself that my life was normal, that everyone lived this way, didn't they? What right did I have to complain? I had everything: a beautiful suburban home, stable jobs, well-behaved children, the quintessential picket fence Yet, each visit to the neighbor's house left me green with envy for the husbands who cherished their wives, the quality time spent with their children, the serene lives they led. But I remained silent; to them, I was no different. I perpetuated the facade, but the charade was more suffocating than the truth itself. I had a husband who drank daily, smoked incessantly, and wore his bad attitude like a badge of honor.

It may have looked picture-perfect from the outside, but the reality was far from it. Deep down, I knew it, but I refused to acknowledge it.

I wish I could say my drinking ended when I left him, but that would be a lie. In truth, it only escalated, spiraling out of control. I found myself consuming a quart of Tito's every few days, my memory fading, my hair thinning, my body bruising easily—I barely resembled my former self, trapped in a downward spiral of self-destruction. I was desperate to numb the pain, to escape the suffocating grip of reality. But the more I drank, the more reckless I became, jeopardizing not only my own life but the lives of others around me. I had no regard for my own well-being, careening dangerously close to the edge of oblivion. Yet, I was too blinded by my own self-destructive tendencies to see the precipice before me. It wasn't until one fateful night, when my reckless behavior nearly led to my demise, that I was forced to confront the harsh reality of my addiction. In a moment of sheer desperation, I attempted to fling myself out of a moving vehicle, only to be saved by a thin thread of fabric clinging to my friend's grasp. As the cold realization of my actions washed over me, I found myself sprawled half-naked on my mother's lawn, teetering on the brink of oblivion. It was a wake-up call—a stark reminder of the depths to which I had sunk. The following day, with trembling hands and puffy eyes, I boarded a plane bound for rehab, embarking on a journey of self-discovery and redemption.

For so long, I deluded myself into believing that my drinking was a byproduct of my husband's addiction. But when I could no longer place blame upon him, I was forced to confront the harsh truth—it was a problem that resided within me. I had to choose my hard. I could choose to keep drinking and slowly kill myself or I could wake up and do the work and have a shot at a better life. What hard do you need to choose?

More Red Flags:
1. **Drinking:** The pattern of excessive drinking, both by your husband and yourself, serves as a significant red flag. It not only indicates potential issues with alcohol dependency but also contributes to a toxic environment within the household.

2. **Verbal Abuse & Mistreatment:** The presence of verbal abuse, characterized by demeaning language and mistreatment, is another concerning red flag. No one should have to endure such behavior, as it can have profound negative effects on mental and emotional well-being.

For the longest time, nobody, including myself, realized I was gasping for air. I dimmed my own light to shield myself from the darkness that enveloped me. His blatant disregard for my pain awakened me to a harsh reality. I was alone. Nobody could shine that light for me, I had to do it for myself.

Here's the thing: was he flawed? Absolutely. But was he the root of the problem? No. I had to confront the fact that I neglected my own well-being, stemming from a lack of self-love and self-worth. Fixing myself became imperative before envisioning a brighter future.

Embarking on sobriety became a transformative journey. It compelled me to confront my inner demons and face the ugly truths head-on. I grappled with a torrent of emotions—I cried, and then I cried some more. The agony of confronting my feelings surpassed the challenges of abstaining from alcohol or missing him. For years, I had sought refuge in distractions, whether it was indulging in drinking, eating, or shopping—anything to avoid confronting myself. I had spent a lifetime evading my own truth, ensnared in a cycle of chaos, caretaking, and people-pleasing, all to maintain a facade of comfort and acceptance.

These are the lies I told myself: Sound Familiar?
- "If I'm me, I won't be loved."
- "I don't deserve better."
- "I don't have anything special to offer."
- "I need to please them to love me."
- "I have to be happy to be seen."

I reached a point of profound self-discovery at the age of 40, utterly lost and terrified. Laden with guilt and shame, I grappled with the concept of self-care, a foreign notion to me. Some days, I'd be paralyzed by numbness, sadness, anger, and confusion, grappling with how to proceed. With the support of AA and my sponsor, I learned healthier coping mechanisms—journaling, walking, reaching out for help, and learning to rest. Restlessness and agitation plagued me initially, but gradually, sleep became my refuge, allowing my battered body to recuperate from years of abuse.

> Sobriety became my compass, guiding me
> toward self-discovery one day at a time.

Walking became my sanctuary, a ritual I observed diligently, finding solace in prayer and connection with the universe. I learned to believe in something greater than myself, finding solace in the embrace of God. I also embraced a motto: I refused to let regrets define my life. Instead, I committed to living fully and pursuing everything I wanted to accomplish. Becoming an author happened to be one of those goals.

You know, they say that sometimes you have angels watching over you, and I've been fortunate to have a few good ones by my side over the past several years.

> "There's a choice we have to make in life: to own our story and walk into it, or to live outside of our story, hustling for our worthiness." - Brene Brown

The moments that jolted me awake didn't happen by chance. They occurred because deep down, I knew I was destined for more. As I progressed on my healing journey, I came to understand my true purpose in life was to serve others on their own paths to healing, helping them uncover their self-worth and self-love. I owe so much to the experiences that shook me awake. I know there are countless women out there, just like I used to be, staying small and comfortable to maintain peace, appease others, and avoid their own truths. I'm not here to judge; I've been there. I'm here to offer my presence, to share my stories, in the hopes that they might ignite a spark within you, illuminating a path out of the darkness.

For me, that spark of hope ignited when I tuned into Oprah's podcast. Her words struck a chord deep within me, as though she was speaking directly to my heart and soul. Surrounding myself with inspiring individuals —friends, and mentors, and delving into several personal development books, I so loved—along with receiving unwavering love and support from my mother, all played pivotal roles in my journey. My children, my greatest teachers, have journeyed alongside me, offering love amidst my stumbles in both parenting and life. I instill in them the belief that life isn't defined by what happens to us, but by how we respond. In turn, they teach me about resilience, unconditional love, and unwavering support.

At times, we test the love of others because we struggle to believe we are worthy of it. It took years for me to open up to trust again, and I believe Thomas entered my life to demonstrate that it was possible. He stood by me through the storms, the tears, and the moments of breakdown. Regardless of how I showed up, he embraced me wholeheartedly. The day Thomas came into my life, seeing beyond my pain and loving me through my darkest days, proved to be significant in my healing journey. His presence was truly a blessing and a gift.

Anything is possible when you have the right people there to support you.

We all need that guiding light to illuminate the darkest corners of our being, to awaken parts of ourselves that lie buried beneath the surface. Often, we're too close to our struggles to see them clearly. It doesn't matter what others say or do; until we're ready to hear it or notice it, we remain blind to our own truths. We are our own harshest critics, judging ourselves relentlessly.

What we fail to realize is that everything we need lies within us. When we truly believe this, our entire perception of life shifts. However, we often find ourselves harshly judging our own actions and choices.

The key lies in learning to forgive ourselves, showing

ourselves love, and compassion, and grace. We must acknowledge that we're doing the best we can with the knowledge and resources available to us.

> *As Maya Angelou wisely said, "When we know better, we do better."*

In coaching, one of the fundamental principles I emphasize is the power of changing our thoughts to transform our lives. Our thoughts dictate our emotions, which in turn influence our actions, ultimately shaping the course of our lives. By altering any one of these elements, we can initiate profound shifts for the better. In coaching, let's consider an example of a client struggling with self-doubt and negative thinking patterns. They consistently tell themselves they are not good enough to pursue their dream career. As a result, they feel anxious and fearful whenever they think about taking steps towards their goals. These emotions lead them to procrastinate or avoid opportunities that could help them progress in their desired direction. Through coaching, we work on changing their negative thoughts to positive affirmations. As they start believing in their capabilities and worth, they feel more confident and motivated to take action. This shift in mindset empowers them to pursue their dreams with enthusiasm and determination, ultimately leading to greater success and fulfillment in their professional endeavors.

With my clients, we go through the Relationship Roadmap, which essentially shows them that all roads lead back to themselves. We follow a 4-step process that focuses on:

1. **Mindset:**
   - Awareness – What limiting beliefs, and patterns are present?

- Inner Dialogue: How we talk to ourselves – Get curious
- Exploring emotions – Get in your body.
- Triggers – What is our response to the outside world and our relationships.

2. **Self-Care:**
   - Physical Well-being
   - Emotional Stability and Safety
   - Social Connections
   - Spiritual Nourishment

3. **Skill Building:**
   - Cultivating Self-Trust
   - Effective Communication
   - Establishing Boundaries

4. **Self-Expression:**
   - Setting and Pursuing Goals
   - Taking Purposeful Action
   - Celebrating Achievements
   - Cultivating Positive Habits
   - Managing Time Effectively

My coaching client, Sarah, approached me at her breaking point, engulfed in overwhelming pain and survival mode. The revelation of her husband's affair shattered her world, leaving her in a state of panic and fear, uncertain of how to navigate the unraveling of her life. Struggling to come to terms with this harsh reality, she felt utterly hopeless and devastated. All Sarah desired was the fundamental foundation of a loving, loyal husband who actively contributed to their partnership and family life. Instead, she found herself shouldering the burdens of maintaining their home, caring for their children, and managing finances, while her husband prioritized his career.

The news of her husband's infidelity left Sarah in a state of bewilderment and confusion. Despite her unwavering efforts to be a devoted wife, she grappled with self-blame and internalized the betrayal as her own failing. She struggled to reconcile the idea that she might not be at fault, clinging to the hope that salvaging the marriage was within reach if only she could try harder. Over time, Sarah came to the painful realization that saving their relationship required both parties to acknowledge the underlying issues and commit to individual growth. She learned that she couldn't bear the weight of their marriage's shortcomings alone and that healing required a mutual effort towards self-improvement and accountability.

Sarah and I embarked on a transformative journey through a four-step process (described above), empowering her to recondition her thoughts and embark on the path towards healing, self-love, and confidence.

Sarah is one example of many women who struggle to realize their self-worth. They look outside of themselves for validation and approval. It was not until I started working with Sarah, that she could realize that what she looked for on the outside, she had to find within herself.

We're often fed the Jerry McGuire notion that someone else will "complete us," but the truth is, nobody completes us except ourselves. The fairytale idea of a knight in shining armor swooping in to rescue us belongs solely in fiction—it's not rooted in reality, nor has it ever been.

In a healthy relationship, you're seeking a partner who can enhance your life, like adding creamer to your coffee, but they should never be your entire coffee. It's crucial to understand your own wants and needs and have the ability to communicate them effectively if you hope to build a fulfilling partnership.

People aren't mind readers; they can't discern our desires and requirements unless we explicitly express them. Much of the frustration in relationships arises from the expectation that our partners should inherently know what we want without us articulating it.

This is where self-discovery and understanding our own desires become crucial. It's fundamental. Unfortunately, these concepts aren't typically emphasized in our upbringing. Instead, we're taught to prioritize kindness, respect, and caretaking for others. While these are important values, they can also contribute to the problem. It's a significant factor in why 80% of women struggle with feeling inadequate. When we internalize the belief that we're not enough, it permeates every aspect of our lives. This belief impacts our relationships, careers, and aspirations because ultimately, we tend to settle for what we believe we deserve, rather than what we truly desire and are capable of achieving.

My mission is clear: to empower every woman to cultivate a deep love for herself, from the inside - out! It's a mission born from the realization that, as children, we're taught to be kind, considerate, and mindful of others, but very rarely are we instructed on the art of self-love and self-care. Much like you, I grew up believing that everyone and everything else should always come before me. It was a pattern that I followed until I found myself overwhelmed, utterly exhausted, and with nothing left to give. It was then that I had to put down the Superwoman cape I'd worn for so long and embrace a new way of living. The challenge lay in not knowing what that new way entailed, or how to embark upon it, beyond the occasional night of quiet reflection or a soothing bubble bath.

I felt lost, scared, and uncertain about the path ahead. Yet, I took one small step after another, slowly but surely finding my way. Now, I'm here to guide you on this transformative journey. Together, we can shift from feeling trapped, overwhelmed, and perpetually putting others first to a life where you are in complete alignment with your true self. You'll learn to identify your desires and the steps to manifest them. You'll confidently say "NO" to what doesn't serve you, knowing it only leads down a path you've outgrown. You'll stop tolerating nonsense, and you'll step into your power, firmly in control of your life.

You take no shit and stop playing small. You are in charge of your life and for once, you'll feel really damn good about it!

When I was lost and uncertain of my identity, I settled for less than I deserved in every facet of my life. My story could have unfolded in two ways: I could have remained in that comfort zone, enduring misery, or I could have taken the brave step to leave and embark on a journey of self-discovery, paving the way for a brighter future for myself and those around me. Thankfully, I chose the path of growth and transformation.

Even amidst my most challenging days now, they pale in comparison to the struggles of my past. It took time, but I eventually found peace within myself. My joy is no longer found in material possessions or temporary distractions; instead, it emanates from simple pleasures like sipping coffee while witnessing the sunrise, witnessing the beauty of nature, and cherishing genuine moments of connection with others. For the first time, I truly understand what it means to live.

> *"The ultimate practice of self-love is perfectly balancing what you need today with what your future self needs tomorrow." - Roxi Nafousi*

If you're feeling stirred by my words, know that I empathize with your journey. I've navigated through similar emotions, grappling with the need to make sense of it all and find clarity. It's a delicate dance we engage in with ourselves, especially as we approach moments of transformation and growth. You don't have to face this journey alone. Whether you need a listening ear or a supportive presence, don't hesitate to reach out. Whether it's picking up the phone or sending an email, I'm here for you. Your story is important, and I genuinely want to hear from you!

Your story matters. Don't ever underestimate the power of your voice, your experiences, and your journey!

Meet Elizabeth Foster, Founder of 'For the Love of Self' Coaching and Podcast Host of The Self-Love Lounge, who is a passionate advocate for self-love and empowerment and is on a mission to ignite inner transformation. With a background in Transformative Self-Love Coaching, Elizabeth is dedicated to helping individuals silence their inner critics and embrace their true worth. She invites readers on a journey of self-discovery and growth, offering practical strategies to conquer self-doubt and cultivate unshakeable confidence. Elizabeth has ramped up her career quickly and continues to grow an amazing audience with a blend of wisdom, compassion, and actionable advice, Elizabeth empowers readers to rewrite their inner narratives and live authentically. Get ready to embark on a journey towards self-love and fulfillment with Elizabeth as your trusted guide!

Elizabeth resides in Wilmington, NC, with her fiancé, son, and beloved fur baby, Cider. While her daughter calls Nashville home, Elizabeth's mothers are nearby in Wilmington. She finds joy in reading, immersing herself in nature, exploring new destinations, and cherishing moments with her family.

Social Media: elizabeth_fortheloveofself/

Email: **elizabeth@fortheloveofself.coach**

Website: https://fortheloveofself.coach/

Podcast: Apple Podcast: **https://podcasts.apple.com/us/ podcast/the-self-love-lounge/id1723415410**

GREG SPILLER: "WHAT HAPPENED TO MY INTERNET?"

There I was, at my desk, on the job, monitoring streaming media content on the network when I noticed heavy pixelation in the video and severe audio disruption in the program broadcast. We called these distorted sounds 'doing the robot' because of the oddly relatable similarity to robot noises from the movies.

It was my job to pay attention to these things, document the event in real time, and escalate reporting to higher level engineers. Such defects in service were anticipated as a possibility and protocols were put in place to react and restore service back to normal. This time was different. It wasn't just me that noticed this with my own assigned programs; everyone else was having the same issue with theirs, too. It was more severe than any of us on the team had seen before.

Being the curious person that I am, I asked around to enough people engaged at the right levels about the root cause of this largescale service disruption. It was shared with me that the official cause was identified as *solar flares*.

In previous technical support roles, I had seen lazy technicians give the masked and false excuse of 'solar flares' to their non-technical customers as the reason for internet network issues. I knew then as I knew now that this was a terrible excuse, especially for internal tracking of the issue by highly skilled engineers and stakeholders.

I immediately called 'bullshit!' to my manager and co-worker friend, then shared past experiences of technicians using this lazy excuse to not address and resolve the actual network problems.

I was determined to prove I was right, and immediately went to search the internet to disprove that *solar flares* were actually causing this disruption. Think about it: if there was a blast from the Sun strong enough to reach the surface of the Earth, and it is essentially an ElectroMagenetic Pulse, wouldn't other electronics be affected just as much? Like my workstation PC and my smartphone?

When I found a news article online from that day[1], I immediately had egg on my face in embarrassment. OK, this time network problems were legitimately caused by solar flares.... (scientifically called a Coronal Mass Ejection.) I shared the update that I had found with my manager and co-worker. I hate having to eat my words and admit I was wrong after calling bullshit.

First, I was gently reminded that, oh yeah, we're whirling around on a big wet rock.

Second, I imagined and visualized in my mind's eye what would happen if the internet stopped, and we lost all powered devices.

I then had an epiphany: due to the intensity and scale of this event, we were almost knocked back to the 3rd Century permanently [2]. These same words fell out of my mouth in this moment of realization. We dodged a HUGE electromagnetic proverbial bullet this time.

A coldness of panic and dread rushed over me like being

kicked into the deepest part of the sea.

I had to find a way to let more people know this happened, because knowing what could happen next was making me fearful of a dystopian aftermath.

I determinedly had the vision of a call to action. Ask everyone that I can reach: Are you aware, and are you prepared? But where do I start?

What is known about Coronal Mass Ejections, and exactly how powerful was this one that was so intense to disrupt services to this degree? What would happen if lights went out, and we then had to survive afterwards in a new, harsh, primitive construct?

What is known about Coronal Mass Ejections?

"Nowadays the National Oceanic and Atmospheric Administration uses the Geomagnetic Storms scale to measure the strength of solar eruptions. The "G scale" has a rating from 1 to 5 with G1 being minor and G5 being extreme. The Carrington Event (1859) would have been rated G5.

Today, a geomagnetic storm of the same intensity as the Carrington Event would affect far more than telegraph wires and could be catastrophic. With the ever-growing dependency on electricity and emerging technology, any disruption could lead to trillions of dollars of monetary loss and risk to life dependent on those systems. The storm would affect a majority of the electrical systems that people use every day.[3]

A massive eruption of solar material, known as a Coronal Mass Ejection or CME, was detected escaping from the Sun at 11:36 p.m. EDT on March 12, 2023."

"The CME erupted from the side of the Sun opposite Earth. While researchers are still gathering data to determine the source of the eruption, it is currently believed that the CME came from the former active region AR3234. This active region was on the Earth-facing side of the Sun from late February through early March, when it unleashed fifteen moderately intense M-class flares and one powerful X-class flare.

Based on analysis by NASA's Moon to Mars Space Weather Office, the CME was clocked traveling at an unusually fast 2,127 kilometers (1,321 miles) per second, earning it a speed-based classification of a R (rare) type CME.

A representation of the CME below shows the blast erupting from the Sun (located at the middle of the central white dot) and passing over Mercury (orange dot.) Earth is a yellow circle located at the 3 o'clock position. "Even though the CME erupted from the opposite side of the Sun, its impacts were felt at Earth."[4]

Credit: NASA's M2M Space Weather Office

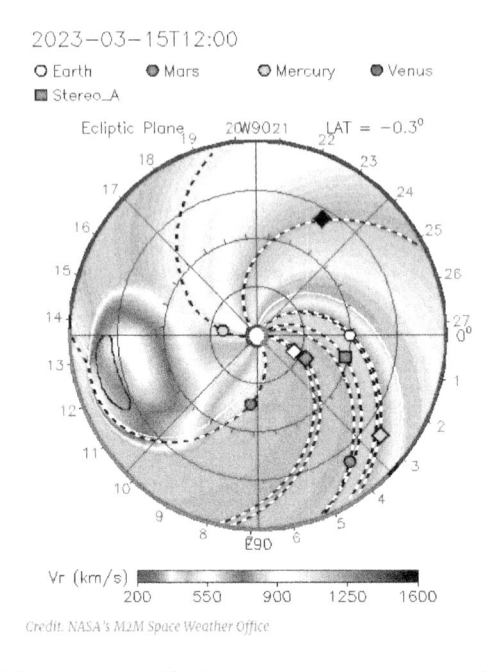

What would happen if lights went out, and we had to survive in a harsh primitive construct?

First, we need to understand how the infrastructure is built, and how we are integrated with it.

The American National Standards Institute/Telecommunications Industry Association (ANSI/TIA) 942 standard covers the telecommunications infrastructure, the power infrastructure, the mechanical infrastructure, the architecture, the fire protection, security, and the monitoring of information centers (including regular office spaces)[5]. These standards shape how the facilities that enable the internet (and also the ones we work in) are built and operated.

In addition, the national power grid is detailed through similar standards and regulatory codes directed by the

National Electrical Code (NEC.)

These are all highly technical, highly detailed engineering programs that fold in civil engineering of commercial and residential communities, small and large. We've all been to a city and live in a neighborhood, right?

Now imagine if ALL power went out, and emergency services that were built (and we depend on) suddenly no longer functioned or mattered?

I am taken back to my time spent as a young man in the Boy Scouts of America program. I was engaged, learned, grew with, and enjoyed Scouting immensely. The Troop I belonged to were all of my friends and classmates from school; meeting up for Scouts was like an extension of palling around together just as we did in the schoolyard and in the neighborhood.

One of the first things you are taught, and is ingrained into your mindset, is the official motto: BE PREPARED.

Another thing that is an integral part of a Scout's journey is the official Handbook. Since its first edition, the Boy Scout Handbook was published to be the primary reference for Scouts. It was used by Scouts at a time when the internet was not available and included practical information a Scout needed. It was and still is brought out of the classroom and into the field including on camping outings. Standard Scouting skills include knife and axe use, map and compass work, knot tying, first aid, shelter building, and many other things one would need to operate in different wilderness landscapes. It is a great reference to have handy and accessible.

Any Scout should know, and it is noted that "in short, to be a good Scout is to be well-developed, well-informed"[6].

In addition, the **Occupational Safety and Health Administration** of the federal government has created an emergency action plan that covers designated actions people must take to ensure safety from fire and other emergencies.

Compiling an emergency action plan is a good way to protect yourself and others during an emergency. They have a downloadable PDF that is an easy read to help understand how you should get to safety quickly in an emergency[7].

How to survive an ElectroMagnetic Pulse: a pocket reference guide

"An electromagnetic pulse, or EMP, is a sudden burst of energy that travels through the air and disables electronics.

The US military and a variety of government agencies have sounded the alarm about the danger to modern life posed by EMPs from three main sources, in reports and studies going back decades: nuclear explosions, severe solar events, and dedicated EMP bombs and sci-fi weapons.

If there were to be an EMP attack, many people would be left without power and access to critical services. An EMP can affect electronic devices and power grids, but it can also cause damage to buildings and homes. Here are some potential effects an EMP could have on your house:

- *Damage to Electrical Systems:* An EMP can damage or destroy electronic devices and electrical systems, including those in your

home. This includes appliances, heating and cooling systems, lighting, and security systems.
- *Disruption of Communications:* An EMP can disrupt communication systems, including phone and internet services. This can make it difficult to contact emergency services or stay in touch with loved ones.
- *Fire Hazards:* An EMP can cause power surges that can overload electrical circuits and start fires. This can pose a serious hazard to your home and personal safety.
- *Structural Damage:* Depending on the intensity of the EMP, it could potentially cause structural damage to your home, such as cracks in walls or damage to the roof.
- *Water and Food Storage:* An EMP event can disrupt the supply chain, making it difficult to obtain food and water. It's important to have a plan in place for storing water and non-perishable food items in case of an emergency."[8]

We should adopt the mindset of a Survivalist to prepare ourselves in the event of a solar Coronal Mass Ejection and/or ElectroMagnetic Pulse at a catastrophic scale.

After developing an immediate safety plan, a good place to focus next is putting together a 'Bug Out Bag'. Many factors come into play when you are building a bug out bag. The first thing you need to consider are your physical limitations. How heavy of a load can you carry for a long distance?

When putting together your bug out bag, be sure to test

your equipment so that you know it will hold up when you need it. When deciding what to put in your pack, follow the Rules of Three when it comes to priority.

You should prioritize finding resources in:
- 3 minutes before needing air (first aid, respirators, face mask, gas mask)
- 3 hours being exposed to the elements (shelter, clothing and fire)
- 3 days without water (water purification and fire)
- 3 weeks without food (food and anything you need to gather and prepare it)

Here are some first aid items you should consider putting in your bug out bag:

MEDICATION:
Prescription medications, aspirin, ibuprofen, anti-diarrheal, antihistamines, Sudafed, multi-vitamins, Epipen (if you have severe allergies), antibiotic ointment, antacids.

BANDAGES:
Band-Aids, butterfly stitches, gauze, ace bandage, triangle bandage, first aid tape, trauma pads, eye patch..etc. You get the idea here.

BASIC FIRST AID ITEMS:
Examine gloves, tweezers, EMT scissors, eye wash, face mask, antiseptic pads, cold compress, insect sting relief (most of these items you will find in a quality first aid kit.)

ADVANCED FIRST AID:
CAT Tourniquet, QuikClot, Israeli Bandages, decompression needle, suture kit, sutures, scalpel blades, snakebite kit, wire splint, SAM splint

Besides first aid, you may consider getting a gas mask to put in your bag. Should there be riots, there will be tear gas. In case of fires, there will be heavy smoke. Wouldn't you like to be able to keep going while others are choking on toxins?

TAMPONS:
While it is not a bad idea to have these in your kit, they are not intended for medical use.

Prolonged exposure to extreme weather conditions can result in death or the loss of limbs. This is the second most important group of items to add to your Bug Out Bag:

HEAD:
Wool winter cap, balaclava, sunglasses, boonie hat, bandana.

TORSO:
Water wicking shirt, long underwear shirt(thermals), t-shirts, light inner jacket, outer heavy jacket (water resistant), rain jacket (with hood), parka, and (camouflage) poncho for when you do want to hide.

HANDS:
Winter Gloves, leather work gloves, fingerless wool gloves

LEGS:
Heavy duty belt, long underwear, roomy cargo pants (water resistant), rain pants

FEET:
Moisture wicking inner socks, wool outer socks, comfortable hiking boots, water socks (so you don't get your boots wet should you need to cross a river or stream.)

FIRE STARTING TOOLS:
Ferro rod, matches, windproof and waterproof matches, butane lighter, Paracord

Next, consider the bigger picture. Where are you bugging out to? Do you have a predetermined location? Do you have supplies at that location already? More information about bug out bags and the essentials you'll need can be found on the internet[9]. Be sure to understand what you'll need, and get one put together before you need it!

Once you have a safety plan in place, and a bug out bag ready to go, stockpiling food is the next required essential to survival; food supply should be thought about in two parts:

What do I need while mobile?
What do I need for my shelter?

PBS Food has compiled a list of basic tips, supplies and food you'll need for both cases:

BOTTLED WATER:
It is an absolute necessity to have plenty of bottled water on hand. A person can survive for nearly a month without food but will severely dehydrate after 3 days without water. Water can also be beneficial in treating scrapes and bruises along the way. Keep in mind though, it won't help in case of a bite.

ENERGY/CEREAL/GRANOLA BARS:
Some combination of energy bars, cereal bars or granola bars is a must have. Anyone prepared should have cases of these in the pantry – they are packed full of energy and nutrients, last basically forever, and travel extremely well.

NUTS/PEANUT BUTTER:
You'll get great nutritional value out of nuts, specifically almonds, walnuts and pecans. Nuts are nutritionally important for their antioxidants, omega-3s, and protein. They are small and easy to transport. Packed with protein, peanut butter doesn't require refrigeration and can be added to less desirable foods to make them taste better, or eaten by itself. Did you know you can also use peanut butter as a natural greasy oil?

CANNED/JERKED MEAT:
Canned/jerked meats are already cooked, processed and ready to eat. They will provide good sustenance and high levels of protein. Canned meats also come in easy to open containers and are often small enough for easy packing and quick consumption. There are many varieties of canned and jerked meat available.

DRIED FRUIT:
Dried fruits are a great source of fiber, anti-oxidants, vitamins and other nutrients like potassium and iron. The best fruits are raisins, cranberries, cherries, currants, and prunes. Dates are high in calories which can serve you well when you need to keep your energy up.

For reference, shelter supplies should last you at least one month and you should have enough food to last you about 2 weeks on-the-run.[10]

Of course, you will need to build temporary and permanent shelters at some point or another. There are 5 basic survival shelters everyone should know[11]. There are plenty of resources available in print and online on how to source material and construct shelters, in a variety of landscapes. Consider where your remote safety location is, and what kind of shelter you will need when you get there.

Would you be able to defend yourself and your loved ones if someone were to physically attack you?

It's a question most of us don't want to consider, but violence is, unfortunately, a fact of life.

Thankfully, regardless of strength, size, or previous training, anyone can learn several effective self-defense techniques[12]. Being able to physically protect and defend yourself will be important during an emergency, especially at a catastrophic scale when mass panic ensues and chaos erupts.

If violence is unavoidable, you'll want to know ahead of time how to fight back effectively—it's possible even against someone bigger or stronger than you. Here are some basic self-defense techniques that can keep you safe:

GET LOUD AND PUSH BACK:
This does two things: it signals for help and it lets the attacker know you're not an easy target.

KNOW THE MOST EFFECTIVE BODY PARTS TO HIT:
Aim for the parts of the body where you can do the most damage easily: the eyes, nose, ears, neck, groin, knee, and legs.

HOW TO MAXIMIZE DAMAGE:
Use your elbows, knees, and head. Use everyday objects. Everyday objects you carry around with you or things in your environment can be used to your advantage as weapons.

LEVERAGE YOUR WEIGHT:
No matter your size, weight, or strength in relation to your opponent, you can defend yourself by strategically using your body and the simple law of physics.

One important group to be aware of, and absolutely need to be prepared for, are known as Marauders. In contrast to 'Preppers' who prepare for extended survival after a mass emergency event, 'Marauders' are a malicious band of thieves that will assault anyone in the nefarious quest to find and obtain resources at any cost, including human life [13].

Being aware that a mass panic emergency event can happen at any time is an important thing to know. If such an event happened at a large enough scale, extended survival will be necessary; most likely in a remote location with limited resources.

Nowadays nearly all of us have the ability to carry an entire library's worth of information around with us in our pockets - and receive timely and important emergency information in ways never even dreamed of less than 25 years ago.

Take advantage of that fact and have a few emergency apps installed on your phone just in case[14]. In your spare time, learn about emergency preparedness so that you can respond immediately, get you and your loved ones to safety, set up a shelter, and be ready for long term survival in a new frontier.

NOTES:
[1] https://talker.news/2023/03/17/huge-doomsday-blast-from-sun-this-week-could-have-killed-earths-internet/
[2] https://historycolored.com/articles/8697/3rd-century-7-historical-events-that-happened-in-the-3rd-century/#:~:text=The%203rd%20century%20was%20dominated,the%20beginning%20of%20its%20end
[3] https://www.freethink.com/energy/solar-storm-46278
[4] https://blogs.nasa.gov/sunspot/2023/03/14/a-powerful-solar-eruption-on-far-side-of-sun-still-impacted-earth/
[5] https://tiaonline.org/products-and-services/tia942certification/ansi-tia-942-standard/
[6] https://www.scoutshop.org/literature.html
[7] https://www.osha.gov/sites/default/files/publications/osha3088.pdf
[8] https://www.thesurvivalprepstore.com/blogs/rants-raves/how-to-survive-an-electromagnetic-pulse-the-ultimate-guide
[9] https://thesurvivaluniversity.com/survival-tips/wilderness-survival-tips/bug-out-bag/
[10] https://www.pbs.org/food/features/13-foods-you-need-to-survive-a-zombie-apocalypse/
[11] https://www.youtube.com/watch?v=tzUpH0Zft5c
[12] https://lifehacker.com/basic-self-defense-moves-anyone-can-do-and-everyone-sh-5825528
[13] https://theprepperjournal.com/2013/11/14/doomsday-preppers-shows-dark-side-of-survival/
[14] https://www.bugoutbagbuilder.com/blog/best-disaster-preparedness-apps

Molded and forged through the Scouting program, **Greg Spiller** is a multi-talented and multi-disciplined professional whose individuality and humanity shines through the prism of Futurism. Entering the Technology space at the emergence of the World Wide Web in the late 90's, his career spans a rich and textured experience across a spectrum of roles and skill sets.

An eternal student of Science, Art, and Philosophy, Greg's curiosity knows no bounds. Altruism and Service are at the forefront of Greg's passion that transfers to motivation and action. A community member that contributes his perspectives, insights, and knowledge to the betterment of us all. Always one to join in the discussion and lend a hand, Greg is on a mission to answer the call to action to make the world a better place. A modern Renaissance Man.

Greg can be found on LinkedIn: https://www.linkedin.com/in/gregory-spiller-80295456/

JAMES MCCONCHIE: "FINDING BALANCE"

L ife is a journey. When you focus on the journey the paths in front of you become clearer. Success in life, for many, has been the focus of the journey itself, not the destination. Here's a small excerpt from some of those catalyst moments on my journey. I hope it offers some insight into your own.

Your journey, with all its side stories and paths, places and people will sometimes write out in your narrative like a movie, where you, the protagonist, are working on the best of your own abilities to get to the positive "end goal." While the story plays out, in your mind you have a specific set of positive outcomes that you will consider successful based on this personal narrative and experiences.

While undertaking the journey of life so many amazing opportunities to learn will arise. That's right, to *learn* and to succeed at whatever challenge is in front of us. There is something beautiful within the human condition; we grow and expand when we do hard things. True growth comes not from success or "winning" but through the trials and tribulations of learning, trying to get better to succeed at your craft whatever it is. When your mind frame shifts from "winning and losing" to "success and learning" the fear of "failure" ceases to exist. There is only opportunity to learn and the opportunity to succeed. When the classic idea of failure is reframed into learning it changes how one might approach difficult situations, that deep inner fear of failure is subdued, because frankly I learned more from "losing" than I ever have from winning.

Keene, New Hampshire, 1982, my story begins with the threads of resilience, nature's embrace, and many unexpected turns in early life. Born amidst the pines and snowflakes of the New England countryside, childhood was "normal" however it was painted with the hues of both challenge and discovery.

At two years old, a diagnosis of spinal meningitis threatened to steal my opportunity in this cycle of life. It was a shitty ordeal that plunged my family into the depths of fear and uncertainty. My equilibrium was off and I was half deaf. Things were going to be challenging; that was the story I was being told.

Thus started my journey trying to find balance through a physical disability.

Southern New England was my sanctuary in my youth, a place where the rustling of leaves and murmuring brooks. Frankly it was pretty Norman Rockwell. It was truly a safe place to grow up, and with that feeling of safety I would find as much time as possible to go hide in the woods. Yes, entitled as fuck. It was here, amidst the ancient elm trees and shadowed glades of small town New Hampshire, that my path initially intersected with entheogenic plants and fungi..

Balance in Wrestling (10 yrs - 25 yrs)

Youth and high school wrestling embodies the essence of the power of the young, resilience, and the pursuit of balance amidst adversity. In the crucible of the wrestling mat, young athletes confront the physical and mental challenges of the sport, learning invaluable lessons that transcend the boundaries of competition.

Wrestling is more than just a sport; it's a way of life—a testament to the transformative power of discipline, determination, and perseverance. As athletes grapple with opponents on the mat, they also grapple with their own inner dimensions and personal growth, confronting fears, doubts, and limitations in the pursuit of greatness and the literal raising of our hand in winning each match. In reality we always seek progression to get that one edge just to get our hand raised into the air by the referee to say "I won."

At the heart of wrestling lies the concept of "embracing the grind"—the relentless dedication to the daily grind of training, conditioning, and self-improvement. It's about embracing the discomfort, the pain, and the struggle, knowing that true growth lies beyond the boundaries of comfort.

In the pursuit of progression, wrestlers learn to focus not on the outcome, but on the process itself. Success is not measured only in wins and losses, but in the incremental progress made, the lessons learned, and the bonds forged in competition and training.

Through the cannon of high school wrestling, young athletes discover the power of resilience, grit, and determination. They learn to push past their limits, to embrace discomfort, and to persevere in the face of adversity.

Wrestling teaches not only how to compete but also how to live—with integrity, courage, and unwavering determination. Inside this grind is the search of balance amidst the chaos of life, we find solace in the rhythm of the mat, where the struggle itself becomes the path to personal progression and balance.

Balance through music, art, counter-culture

At the age of sixteen, a blaze engulfed my family home, casting shadows of uncertainty over my entire world. In the ashes of destruction, I found solace in the entheogenic substances that promised escape from the harsh realities of existence. Cannabis and mushrooms became recreational allies, offering glimpses of transcendence amidst the chaos of adolescence. My obsession with 1960's counter culture, Led Zeppelin, The Grateful Dead, Ken Kesey (champion High School and college wrestler), Timothy Leary, Andy Warhol, Ram Dass. All these students of life started floating into my world and teaching me as I re-emerged from the fire. The soundtrack and narrative that fascinated my young mind was laying the foundation for my future self.

After the fire, I had to find a way to help self-regulate because the pressure of life was making me feel overwhelmed all the time. Cannabis became a steady ally for my ADD and emotional anxiety.

My academic and athletic life was rigorous within the discipline of wrestling, and the quest for self-discovery through music, art, and as a wrestler was constant, I poured my heart and soul into training, pushing the physical and mental limits in pursuit of excellence on the mat. Yet, beneath the surface, I yearned for more—a deeper understanding of myself and the world around me. As I continued to dive into historical counter-culture, a draw to the center, the apex of this history started to be something I began to dream about: living in a VW bus, on the coast, driving up and down and just living the "California Dream." Little did I know this dream would manifest itself some 10 years later.

My college journey began with aspirations of a conventional path—pursuing a degree in tech and aiming for a "real job." However, fate intervened one day during my freshman year when I stumbled upon a wrestling practice while walking back to the dorm.

As I delved back into the world of wrestling, I realized that the dedication and discipline demanded by the sport mirrored the values essential to my academic pursuits. Despite initial failures and setbacks, there were a lot of failures, to be blunt. The first three years were hard as a college wrestler.

Junior year, I emerged as a formidable force on the mat, my relentless dedication to transforming myself became a beacon for success. The anticipation of a home dual meet against a nationally ranked team electrified me. I was ready. As the match unfolded, I faced my opponent with determination, seizing control of the first period with a display of training and tenacity. Yet, in a climactic twist of fate, a routine maneuver turned disastrous as my opponent executed a dramatic throw, dislocating my collarbone in the process.

I fell into a hole for over six months. The injury set me back mentally and emotionally. In that moment of agonizing defeat, I confronted the harsh reality of my physical limitations. I focused on relieving my mental and physical pain. I fell into the "relief" consuming more and more of whatever substance I could. This created more fog, but thankfully I persisted in finishing college, getting a job, and creating new opportunities to learn.

I worked hard enough through my academic career to be able to move to San Francisco, entering the hottest emerging tech market of the mid 2000's. By the sheer chance my best friend from NH had moved out west to forage her own path and as I started my career.

After college I had to find a way to help self-regulate because the pressure of life was making me feel overwhelmed all the time. Without wrestling, Cannabis became my companion and alcohol became my crutch.

I relocated to San Francisco, embracing the chance to explore personal and spiritual growth alongside my close friend from New Hampshire, "Tank." Tank's open-hearted invitation allowed me to embark on a journey of self-discovery and connection. Together, we delved into alternative lifestyles, uncovering fascinating new perspectives and ways of living.

Within the streets of San Francisco, I found myself immersed in a wide variety of experiences that expanded my horizons. The friendship between myself and Tank became a catalyst for transformation, sparking conversations that challenged beliefs and ignited my personal passion.

San Francisco was my new home. A place of inspiration and hope. This beautiful city by the bay became my new sanctuary.

As I embarked on my journey through the realm of tech I managed, I managed well in many perspectives. I navigated the dizzying heights and pitfalls of the corporate ladder for over a decade. As a corporate employee and an independent contractor, I was able to chart my course through some of the industry's most notable startups.

Yet, beneath the veneer of professional achievement, amidst the hustle and grind of Silicon Valley, I sought solace and connection with my peers through unconventional means, sharing psychedelics and entheogens with my bosses, managers, and coworkers. Through these forays into work/play and the mind's eye I began to acknowledge that taking psychedelics might be good for our general health and that microdosing was more than likely going to be the new caffeine. It really helped me focus.

I lived on the edge of every moment every day. I was disillusioned by the allure of corporate advancement and "staking my claim." Whether mentally, physically or emotionally, all within my professional and personal life, it was all gas and no brakes. When the economy crashed in 2008 so did my career in tech. At the time I was killing it, as a new coach to the sport of HS wrestling, as a corporate employee, and within my personal life and relationships. However, when the economy hit this downturn, I was left in a bind.

Amidst the financial crisis in America, I pressed myself to go back to school in 2010. Again, the concept of learning and pursuing my love for the outdoors, the ever-recurring theme in my life. I wanted to design technical apparel and backpacks. I started taking classes in fashion design so I could learn how to sew. I was spending as much time as possible outdoors skiing, climbing, surfing, and camping while my tech-life was on hiatus. Life at this time was focused on getting outside and being in nature.

In 2011, while pursuing my outdoor apparel goals, working through my sewing curriculum, I happened to sit directly across from this beautiful woman. For context, the classroom/workshop consisted of 10 industrial sewing machines across the entire length of the huge classroom, and 40 students distributed amongst those ten machines. It was pure chance the day we happened to be sitting across from each other.

A year after we had our first connection across the sewing machines, we reconnected through Facebook on a simple post about losing my wallet. She told me to sew a pink sparkly one, then I asked her on a date.

Six months later, in 2012, we eloped and got married in San Francisco city hall. Two years later our son, Sydney, was born. Is that a short time? Yes, and it was the best decision of my life. Melinda came into my world at the right time, and so did Sydney. We started planning for our future together. Life was perfect.

Six months after Sydney was born, Melinda felt an abnormal lump in her breast. That moment would be a huge defining factor of our relationship over the next few years. Melinda was diagnosed with Stage 2B (AAA+) Breast Cancer. Thus began another journey that, from afar, was the scariest thing either of us had undertaken.

We formed a united front. We would learn as much about

her cancer and find as many alternative modalities that would complement her chemo and radiation treatment.

Paul Stamets, famed mycologist and mushroom scientist, has been an advocate for mushrooms for decades. He owns one of the largest mushroom product companies (Fungi Perfecti), owns many patents, and is known as "the mushroom man" with the signature hat made out of mushrooms. In 2010, Paul's mother was diagnosed with Stage 4B breast cancer at 80 years old. A 4B diagnosis is considered terminal. When going through treatment options the idea of consuming the "turkey tail" mushroom to help boost immune system response became a part of her treatment. She overcame her Stage 4 diagnosis and showed no signs of cancer after her chemo/radiation in conjunction with consuming a consistent amount of the turkey tail mushroom. *Whoa, we're doing this,* was our shared response. At the same time, Johns Hopkins University began its breakthrough research on the use of Psilocybin Mushrooms for PTSD, trauma, and palliative care. A joke came about in conversation about the turkey tail, and how psilocybin might be another mushroom to add. Little did I know this joke would be the next step to my personal balance.

The next year consisted of a weekly treatment of about 800 milligrams of turkey tail daily, navigating my young parenthood, a reentry into tech to help cover our insurance costs, and watching my partner battle with the side effects of the drugs and treatment. Surprisingly, the turkey tail seemed to help. Melinda was able handle the aggressive chemo and radiation with barely any side effects. *Wow,* I thought, *mushrooms are more than just a side dish, they truly are medicine.* However, purchasing the monthly amount of turkey tail from Stamets at this daily level wasn't very cost effective. While walking the dogs in the park one day I noticed what I thought might be a turkey tail mushroom. This spun my mind. Mushrooms were so avidly in my thoughts that I began to explore the forest floor more closely.

After breaking the veil of finding my first turkey tail mushrooms in Golden Gate Park in 2016, I started to see the full fungal universe that surrounded me and my environment. This motivated me to dive completely into the world of mycology through YouTube and Stamets' Books. I was learning from some amazing people (Willy Myco, Roger Rabbit, Doma Nunzio.) Just by watching and asking questions online I became immersed in the cultivation community.

Through the same grind and effort with years of wrestling, I started the process of learning how to cultivate my own mushrooms. Within six months I was teaching my friends, sharing the benefits of medicinal, culinary, and psilocybin mushrooms. I began growing all mushrooms and sharing the turkey tail I had grown with Melinda.

Melinda's treatment finished in late 2016 and one of the hard facts of cancer is once you're done with treatment, you're not done with cancer. You have to wait, and in our case that wait was over a year to see if her cancer was in remission. At this time my job in tech was overbearing. I continued to climb the corporate ladder however I wasn't happy with the direction I had chosen, and I started to flail under the pressure and anxiety. The uncertainty of Melinda's prognosis was eating at my soul.

Enter microdosing psilocybin. I was dealing with the pressures of work and anxiously awaiting to hear if Melinda was in remission when the Johns Hopkins study popped back into mind one day as I was searching for psilocybin mushrooms. Shortly after finding my first psilocybe in the wild, I began cultivating and microdosing lion's mane and psilocybin. I started this microdosing protocol based on some of the things I heard from Dr. Jim Fadiman, Stamets, and other researchers. This was profound! My fear and anxieties became more manageable, and my sense of balance within life was visible, in spite of the uncertainty. I felt ready to take on any further challenge.

2017/18. Melinda was declared to be in full remission from her breast cancer. As of 2024 she is still in remission. Thank you, mushrooms.

Blessed by the universe, a storefront workshop on the street level of our apartment building opened up and we took a chance. In 2018, Melinda and I opened the Haight Street Shroom Shop. We rented it with the idea that mushrooms were becoming a more important part of our society. This was a space for me to expand my work, educational workshops, and advocacy work. In 2019 I left working in tech completely and since then have enjoyed teaching people about growing mushrooms at home, how to develop their own microdosing protocols, and working as a political advocate for the decriminalization of entheogenic plants and fungi.

In 2022, myself, along with DecrimSF brought forward broad deprioritization language to the San Francisco Board of Supervisors who *unanimously voted to deprioritize entheogenic plants and fungi for personal use* in the city of San Francisco.

In 2024, the shop still sits right in the heart of San Francisco, about 2 blocks away from the iconic corner of Haight & Ashbury at 2080 Hayes Street. Come say Hi, and let's find your mushroom recipe for balance.

"Myco" James McConchie is a mycology and psychedelic educator, decriminalization advocate, and founder of the Haight Street Shroom Shop in San Francisco CA. HSSS is the country's first educational workshop space dedicated to mycology and psychedelic education. James also hosts the Psychedelic Coffee Shop, a live forum podcast discussion with industry professionals and community members on the current state of psychedelics. Additionally, James is also a cofounder of decrimSF.org. Which successfully brought forward broad decriminalization/deprioritization language in September 2022 (resolution #220896). A unanimous decision was granted by the San Francisco board of supervisors to decriminalize personal use, cultivation and sharing of entheogenic plants, cacti and fungi in the city of San Francisco.

W: www.haightstshroomshop.com
Podcast: https://podcasts.apple.com/us/podcast/psychedelic-coffee-shop/id1721632971
IG: www.instagram.com/haightstreetmush (new sep 2023)
In (personal) https://www.linkedin.com/in/jamesmcconchie/
FB: www.facebook.com/haightstshroomshop

ALAN CHAPMAN: "PEACE IS NOW"

The purpose of this information is to plant seeds and open doors so that you can re-imagine a new reality for yourself, using any or all of the ideas offered.

Have you ever imagined a different reality?

Have you ever imagined a different reality and actually made it real?

Would you like to?

If so, try this.

Relax your jaw. Relax your shoulders. Breathe more slowly and deeply.

Breathe in, slowly and deeply, from your stomach, through your nose preferably, then exhale through your mouth, slower than your inhale.

Are your jaw and shoulders relaxed?

Notice what you are noticing. Become more aware of your awareness.

Feel the sensations of your body.

Especially feel tensions relaxing in your face, jaw, neck, scalp, forehead, shoulders.

Let's call this a 'practise.'

Do all this practise for about a minute, longer if you wish.

Don't do it while you're driving or operating dangerous machinery, or up a ladder. That's a serious piece of humour, because it's easy to become so relaxed that you'll fall asleep, and sleep is a separate subject for later.

Do this practise from memory without having to hold this book or your e-book reader.

Do it sitting comfortably so you can relax completely, lying down on your back on a bed or yoga mat or carpet.

Or if it's warm and dry enough, do it outside, perhaps on a beach or on a lawn, with the sky above. Or lay a blanket on the ground.

Daylight is hugely helpful for your circadian rhythm (your natural sleep patterns) and your hormone melatonin, from your pineal gland. Circadian is from Latin, circa, meaning *approximately*, and dies, meaning *day*. Circadian refers to the natural 'body-clock' of animals and plants of about 24 hours.

If you can hear birds chirping this is good too, because birds chirp when they feel safe. This helps increase our own feelings of safety, peace and calm.

Night time is good too, looking at the stars. Avoid bright lights at night, especially LEDs. Candle-light is, as well.

Let your limbs feel weightless. They need no support from your mind and body.

Now ask yourself, in your head or out loud, "Have I ever imagined a different reality?"

And there, you just did.

Practise this calming exercise any time you can and want. It's free.

The more you practise, the more you 'rewire' your neural circuitry.

Habits are a 'practise' of repeating and reinforcing neural circuitry, for positive healthy or negative unhealthy outcomes.

Do you see? You can change your feelings and physiology by changing how you use your body.

Also, you can change your feelings and physiology by changing what you put into your body.

This becomes more wonderful when you realise that REAL FOOD tastes so much better than the poisonous rubbish of ultra-processed food and drinks (UPFs.)

Ultra-processed food and drinks (UPFs)

"You are what you eat, and drink"

Ultra-processed foods and drinks are not 'real food' nor 'real drinks.'

UPFs contain toxic chemicals and far too much sugar.

Many experts in addictions consider sugar to be the 'gateway drug' to all other addictions.

I understand this because I'm a member of the International Food Addiction Consensus. Compared to most people, including doctors, I'm highly trained and qualified in nutrition and metabolic health.

Metabolism refers to the processes in a living organism necessary to maintain life, from Greek metaballein, meaning *to change*.

Your physiology is constantly changing, depending on your nutrition and lifestyle. Physiology refers to how living organisms function.

UPFs damage your microbiome. Your microbiome is your 'gut' or more technically your intestines, and the 'gut flora' or healthy bacteria or microbes necessary for good metabolic health, including healthy sleep.

Remind yourself that you are a whole connected system.

Ask yourself," How well do I sleep? Do I wake refreshed?"

Sleep

Sleep is when and how your mind-body system processes and heals your day's physical and emotional exertions.

If we do not sleep well, then we do not maintain good health.

Our sleep is worsened by many unhealthy things, for example UPFs (ultra-processed foods and drinks), EMR (electromagnetic radiation), EMF (electromagnetic field) radiation, blue and white light such as screens and LED lights shortly before bedtime.

Night-shift working and jet-lag are other examples of unhealthy impacts on sleep.

Stress, grief and trauma are other damaging impacts on sleep.

Stress, grief and trauma also create a need for more sleep.

Too much alcohol impacts our sleep, and destroys microbiome (gut flora), which in turn impacts health and sleep.

Eating too late before bedtime disrupts sleep, and hinders brain and body recovery and healing.

Good sleep is necessary for reducing inflammation.

You can understand these many connected causes and effects as 'feedback loops.'

Ask yourself: "What 'feedback loops' might be upsetting my metabolic health?"

Ask yourself, "What opportunities do I have for reversing these feedback loops to improve my metabolic health?"

Nutrition

There is vast evidence now that high-carbohydrate ('carbs') foods and drinks are extremely unhealthy.

Carbs turn to glucose (sugar) in our blood. Rice, potatoes and processed cereals (pasta) are mostly carbs.

The more processed a food or drink is, then the less healthy it is.

This is logical and common sense when you consider how you are evolved and designed to live, over thousands of years.

Humans have only had processed foods for a few generations. Low-fat anything is unhealthy. Grain, seed and vegetable oils are also very unhealthy.

While every human is different, there are some firm limits beyond which nearly every human will become metabolically unwell.

Given the questionable ethics of our governments and health authorities, and of multinational corporations of pharmaceuticals and ultra-processed foods and drinks, ask yourself, "Do I see a connection between all these factors, so my health and longevity are being damaged, because big businesses and politicians are more interested in profit than in my wellbeing and the wellbeing of my children?"

Our ancestors a few generations ago worked outdoors in daylight and sunlight. Chemicals, now poisoning our foods and drinks, did not exist.

The meats, fruits and vegetables that we ate throughout most of our evolution were more naturally reared, produced, grown and harvested. There was no intensive farming; no food factories.

The agricultural revolution happened around the world about 10,000-15,000 years ago. Before about 100,000 years ago, humans were mostly hunter-gatherers. Diets were natural for local regions and communities, aligned with lifestyles of outdoor life, work and play, song and dance, without smartphones and modern technologies.

People's nutritional needs were met by what their local environment provided. There were no supermarkets nor take-away restaurants nor deliveries.

Fruit and vegetables were not selectively or genetically modified to be sweeter, as is the case nowadays.

Twenty-first century foods, drinks and lifestyles are mostly 'monoculture' wherever you visit in the world. It's industrialised farming and food production on a global scale, and people use the same smartphones and tend to live and work indoors, or driving cars and vans etc., mostly sitting down.

As a species we have mostly become addicted to convenience.

Ask yourself, "What do I know about addictions? What do I crave? What do I eat and drink that gives me a short-term 'pleasure hit' and then I want more of it?"

The purpose of this information is not to suggest an optimal human diet and lifestyle, because each of us is different. Also we are limited by our circumstances; but only up to a point. We actually have vast freedoms and flexibilities by which to question, inform ourselves, and experiment with our own ideal diet and lifestyle.

The purpose of this information is to plant seeds and open doors so that you can re-imagine a new reality for yourself, using any or all of the ideas offered.

Addictions

Addiction is a highly complex subject. Research into what drives addictions is a very new and fast-emerging area of study and therapy.

Factors influencing addictions include birth, parenting,

education, injury, abuse, disease, work, stress, lifestyle.

There are many more.

Generational trauma is a major factor (see below.)

Ask yourself, "What do I know about my own traumas?"

If you are happier not asking and not knowing, that's fine, too. For many people this can be a very good approach: to believe that the past has gone and cannot be changed; what matters is what you change now; so the future becomes your new reality.

In my own experience, awareness and information are crucial for empowering transformational action.

In order to change something, we must first become aware that it can be changed. If you are unaware that something can be changed then perhaps you are dependent on some other intervention; passive rather than proactive.

Personally, I like the empowerment approach. But each of us is different.

It seems from emerging research that humans are 'hard-wired' to be addicted, from very ancient times when food was not plentiful. We needed 'triggers' for our brains to remind us where animals and other foods could be trapped, hunted and foraged.

Put simply, big business has worked out over many decades how to exploit these triggers to sell more of everything to us all, for profit. Neuro-marketing.

A way to understand how these triggers happen in our brains and sensory circuitry, is when we see our kitchen, home or workplace, we are reminded, prompted (triggered) to want a cup of tea or coffee (caffeine is addictive), often with milk and sugar, both sweet. Sweetness is additive. When we make our tea or coffee, we see the biscuit tin or some cake, and this triggers us again.

Rituals and habits are part of addictions.

Remember that habits are a 'practise' of repeating and reinforcing neural circuitry, for positive healthy or negative unhealthy outcomes.

Ask yourself, "What habits and rituals do I have that could be reinforcing unhealthy lifestyle and nutrition?"

Addictions are not limited to foods and drinks.

Addictions tend to shift from one to another.

For example it is common for people trying to give up smoking to over-eat and drink the wrong (addictive) ultra-processed foods and drinks, so putting on weight.

Shopping is for many people an addiction, so is hoarding, collecting, gambling, cleaning, alcohol, recreational drugs, painkillers, antidepressants and more. It's a very long list.

Some believe that a disease-approach to addiction is good for treatment; others disagree.

I suspect that whatever works best for people, is best.

If it helps you to believe that you are an incurable alcoholic so abstinence forever is the best answer then that's okay for you.

If it helps you to believe that you can cure your alcoholism so that you can take an alcoholic drink again occasionally without falling back into addiction, then that's okay for you, too.

From my decades of binge-drinking ridiculous amounts of alcohol, I cured my addiction completely. It took me about 15 years. So now I can have an occasional alcoholic drink if I choose, but I choose not. I'd rather have a cup of tea.

Generational trauma

Remind yourself, "What does not kill me makes me stronger," (I'm paraphrasing Friedrich Nietzsche.) Dark switches to light when you realise the reality you can create.

Generational trauma is profoundly significant.

Suicides 'cluster' partly or mainly because of this. Same with abuse of all sorts.

It's about learned conditioned behaviours. It's complex, deep, and particularly so from the female perspective.

I recommend very strongly the book *The Wise Wound* by Penelope Shuttle and Peter Redgrove (1978-2015 revisions.) It's beautifully written because the co-authors are award-winning poets.

Detailing or summarising *The Wise Wound* book is beyond the scope of my writings here, except to say that the subjugation and traumatising of women and girls, is a genocide ongoing that has been happening for thousands of years, much related to men's fears and distortions of menstruation.

It is possible easily with a little research to discover vast brilliant works explaining generational trauma.

It's less easy to find great works about menstruation and its meaning for humankind because the subject remains such a taboo.

In my own very deep lived experience of suicidal disintegration and spiritual rebirth, the work of Kazimierz Dabrowski and William 'Bill' Tillier - https://www.positivedisintegration.com/ - Theory of Positive Disintegration (TPD) - explains 'the point of the pain' and how we can grow via trauma. TPD is much more. Bill Tillier's paper on realities at the 1996 Dabrowski Congress (https://alanchapman.substack.com/p/realities-plasma-energies-william) aligns with the plasma energies work of Robert Temple; is implicit in Graham Hancock's work; and in Gill Edwards' books (Living Magically, etc.) These are different perspectives on energies beyond physical realms.

Education and training of doctors and 'health professionals'

Internationally, various terms describe doctors working in primary or general treatment, notably: primary care physician, family physician (USA), GP or general practitioner (UK.) Elsewhere, medical officer, registered medical practitioner.

Additionally, there are very many other health professionals such as psychiatrists, psychologists, surgeons, midwives, etc. Of special note: gynecologists who are men. What's that all about, if not perversion and worse?

Most health professionals are taught at university, to diagnose illness and prescribe pharmaceuticals and surgical interventions.

Training in nutrition is almost zero. In the UK it's just a few hours. This outrage is prevalent wherever big business influences educational institutions. Medical doctors of all sorts are incentivised to prescribe pharmaceuticals and other clinical interventions.

Ask yourself, "Who funds universities, and why?"

Ask yourself, "Does this feel right? Do I smell a rat?"

Ask yourself, "What opportunities do I have to inform myself about my health, free from bias and vested interests?"

Ask yourself, "When does this education towards a prescription-based health economy begin? Does this affect my children? What can I do to improve the situation?"

Holistic health

Holistic means 'whole system' from the word holism, a term from the 1920s used by some psychologists and philosophers interested in metaphysics.

Holistic medicine refers to treating the whole system of a human, or animal, considering connections with nature and sunlight, etc., rather than a profit-medicine approach based on treating symptoms.

'Metaphysics' dates back to ancient Greece and Plato: the study of what transcends 'physical' realities, which includes notions of heaven and faith.

Holistic health includes treatments such as herbal medicine, psychedelic therapies, reiki, walking in nature, gardening, acupuncture, reflexology, lymph massage, yoga, pilates, mindfulness, meditation, and/or simply nutritional changes.

Nowadays holistic medicine is commonly called 'alternative.' A few generations ago our modern 'western' profit-medicine approach was called 'alternative.'

Modern medicine is additionally profitable for corporations because the medicated are then prescribed more drugs and surgery as their conditions worsen.

Holistic medicine treats causes of ailments and disease, aiming to restore a natural balance of metabolic health to prevent disease occurring. Vast amounts of holistic medicine is completely free, via free educational information.

Modern medicine's strategy is to fix acute illness, for example after a heart attack, but then to prescribe more drugs.

Holistic health aims to prevent illness.

Ask yourself, "What health or lifestyle issues do I want to improve for myself, my children, my grandchildren?"

Longevity or 'health span'

This refers to our health for our whole life.

Increasingly for the past few generations, chronic diseases

such as diabetes, heart problems, cancers and mental illness occur in the last 30 years of life.

Many people now face serious mental and physical illness challenges in childhood and teenage years.

Inflammation features in all these conditions.

The aim of holistic health is good health for whole life, and to avoid premature preventable death.

Suicides and modern 'western' medicine mistakes are increasingly high and avoidable causes of premature death.

Ask yourself," Why is this happening?"

Might it be happening because modern medicine is based mostly on profit, rather than the prevention of disease using treatments and information which make very little money?

Ask yourself, "What sort of health span do I want for myself?"

Ask yourself, "What sort of health span do I want for my children and grandchildren?"

Ask yourself, "What do I need to know that I don't know yet, about how to understand my 'whole system' health and lifestyle?"

Ask yourself, "What does my genetic ancestry tell me about my ideal diet and lifestyle?"

Ask yourself, "Why do doctors not prescribe building muscle, especially later in life?"

Neuroplasticity

Neuroplasticity is a modern word which means that our brains and entire nervous system (neuro) can change (plasticity.)

You were born with tens of billions of brain cells (neurons.) Each neuron has 15,000 or more connections (synapses) with other brain cells. When you were three years old your brain already had 1000 trillion synapses. (https://www.nature.com/articles/s41380-022-01931-x/)

Animals have neural-circuitry of huge complexity too.

You will find other very credible research supporting this information.

We interact with animals and other people. Remember this when tachyons are explained later.

Human physiology is by definition a connected system internally and externally.

Part of your physiology is your connections with sunlight and nature.

When we eat, drink, and change our breathing and use of our body, we change our neural circuitry, because we are making new synaptic connections.

Happiness and peace are not addictive and are healthy. Mostly happiness and peace are free for us to attain.

Pleasure is addictive and generally unhealthy. Addictions are driven by cravings. We keep doing these unhealthy things because we've been conditioned and triggered by clever advertising and marketing.

Suicide and homicide are examples of the destructive

potential of neuroplasticity. Stress and inflammation combine with other chronic ill-health conditions in a chaotic cocktail of feedback loops and rewiring of our neural circuitry.

Interestingly and naturally, given all the information and evidence offered here, a helpful intervention for depression, anxiety, poor sleep and obesity, is to change diet and lifestyle to be less inflammatory. This naturally begins to reverse the feedback loops so they become healthy rather than unhealthy.

Our minds are magically powerful when we realise this.

For inspiration I recommend the works and teachings of authors and healers who survived the Nazi Holocaust. They teach us about neuroplasticity, forgiveness and humanity very profoundly. By enduring and surviving the greatest traumas imaginable, certain people are able to transcend, and to help others transcend too. You have this potential.

Love

Love is an infinite free source of energy. Enough said.

Tachyons

A tachyon (from the 1960s, and Greek takhus meaning *swift*) is a hypothetical particle in physics that travels faster than the speed of light.

Hold that thought, for a tachyon.

Physics is an attempt to explain energy.

There are other explanations.

The word zeitgeist is from German, zeit, *time*, and geist, *spirit*. Zeitgeist means a mood or feeling among people at a particular time.

Ask yourself, "How does zeitgeist happen?"

Many dog-owners experience their dog being able to sense the owner's feelings. Also, many dogs know when their owners are returning home, when the owners are miles away, completely out of sight and sound range.

Many twins experience awareness of each other's feelings when miles apart, even on different sides of the world.

When you are in a crowd of people, for instance at a sports event, or concert or dance, or in a church singing, there is a collective mood or energy.

Ask yourself, "How is this mood or energy shared?"

Ask yourself, "Why do we say 'gut instinct' and 'gut feeling'?"

When we daydream, our realities alter.

When we dream asleep, our realities change even more. Our altered realities are actually real.

Ask yourself, "Am I open to the possibility that tachyons could be constantly connected energies, which explain energies such as plasma and entanglement theory?"

Ask yourself, "Are we and everything vibrations, rather than solid, liquid and gaseous matter?"

You'll realise by now I believe we all can change and manifest our chosen realities far beyond what we've been taught and conditioned to believe possible.

Peace is now.

What's your reality?

Thank you for reading.

Infinite love, gratitude, abundance to you, and all else beyond peacefully magically beautiful.

Alan

Books and information

Here are just a few of the main books and educational information sources that support my words above. I offer this as information not clinical advice. I could list many dozens of resources. I believe you will find what will help you best by exploring below and much else on my own websites: https://livewildlivefree.org/ and https://alanchapman.com/

https://nutrition-network.org/

https://publichealthcollaboration.org/ (https://phcuk.org/)

https://lowcarbfreshwell.com/

https://www.dietdoctor.com/

https://www.prolongevity.co.uk/ - nutrition and pharmacy

International Food Addiction Consensus Conference - co-leaders/co-founders Clarissa Kennedy and Molly Painschab - https://www.sweetsobriety.ca/ and https://www.unsugaredu.com/

https://www.bittensaddiction.com/ - Bitten Jonsson, food addiction pioneer

https://robertlustig.com/ - Robert Lustig, food addiction pioneer

https://forkintheroad.co.uk/ - Jen Unwin, food addiction pioneer

https://www.diagnosisdiet.com/ - Georgia Ede, nutrition/mental health pioneer

https://www.zoeharcombe.com/ - nutrition expert

https://dreditheger.com/ - The Choice and The Gift - holocaust, forgiveness

The Savage God, Al Alvarez - suicide

The Inflamed Mind, Edward Bullmore - inflammation, suicide

Matthew Walker and Nick Littlehales - sleep

Yes to Life, Victor Frankl (posthumous 2020) in many ways more powerful than his book Man's Search for Meaning. Night, Elie Wiesel (1960.) If This Is A Man (1947) and The Truce (1963), by Primo Levi.

https://drgabormate.com/ - The Myth Of Normal, Gabor Mate and Daniel Mate (2022) - I consider the information about generational trauma to be profoundly brilliant. I believe there is an existential ecosystem challenge far beyond the confusions about 'climate change' and 'global warming.' There is evidence for global cooling soon.

The Wise Wound, Penelope Shuttle & Peter Redgrove (1978-2015 rev) - subjugation of women for millennia, lunar/menstrual cycles, trauma, much more.

https://robert-temple.com/ - A New Science Of Heaven, Robert Temple (2022) - plasma energies, and much more.

https://grahamhancock.com/ - America Before: The Key To Earth's Lost Civilization, Graham Hancock (2019) - energies and much more.

https://www.positivedisintegration.com/ - Kazimierz Dabrowski and William 'Bill' Tillier - trauma, sensitivity, suicidal disintegration and recovery, spiritual growth, energies, realities, and much more.

https://www.bitchute.com/channel/zWFwoSPHMLwa/ - Mark Steele - 5G, nanoparticles, weapon systems, biowarfare.

https://standupwolverhampton.com/ - EMR/EMF Radiation, 5G and related activism

https://warnermendenhall.com/ - legal actions vs covid mandates mostly USA.

https://www.youtube.com/watch?v=X8lEFYvy4qA - Richard Vobes - an example of his profoundly brilliant interviews.

https://rumble.com/user/cbkovess - Medical Doctors for Covid Ethics - extraordinarily powerful educational online meetings

https://alanchapman.substack.com/ - Alan Chapman's substack

https://linkedin.com/in/alchap/ - Alan Chapman's

LinkedIn - and @lifedeathfest twitter and getrr

https://dancegeneration.co.uk/ - Maria Hennings Hunt - co-founder of https://livewildlivefree.org/ and author of IMHO the best adult/children's book ever written, The Lullaby Fairy - https://mariahenningshunt.co.uk/product/the-lullaby-fairy/

https://alanchapman.com/music/ (song #15) - Maria Loony Toons - and https://www.youtube.com/watch?v=OMtGsfJZmvI

When we see the Moon we see that we are connected souls. We are mirrors, amplifying love infinitely.

Alan Chapman is on a mission to manifest peace now, every beautiful moment. The past is gone; the future is our chosen reality from the infinite universes - all inside our heads! Time is illusory. We are pure energy. Conscious subconscious. Soul. Alan is a writer of story songs and uplifting endless optimism. Fearless love and compassion; holistic healing; authentic connectedness: moon, sun, dust, stars, breath, dreams, chakras and chi, herbs in our tea, nature and trees. Alan transitioned via birth in 1957 to corporate multinational leadership and executive coaching, to world-renowned educationalist, then years and layers of traumas and suicidal disintegrations to recovery and spiritual rebirth. Alan lets go what no longer serves him, is a metabolic health coach, member of the International Food Addiction Consensus, and a plasma human being. He is from London, has three grown children and several grandchildren.

See AlanChapman.com and LiveWildLiveFree.org.

LONNEE REY: "ARE YOU A SEEKER OR A BEAKER?"

If you ever wondered about the impact you can have – you just being you, doing life, or having fun the way you do, check this out:

While waiting to use a pinball machine, 25-year-old Roger Sharpe saw a player do something he'd never seen before: instead of using the flippers to bang wildly at the pinball with random target hits, he used them to stop and cradle the ball. He was then able to control the direction and skilfully aim the ball at high-point targets. It was no longer a game of chance, but rather one of skill and strategy.

This may not seem significant, but it ended-up flipping the script, overturning a ridiculous ruling:

For over three decades, pinball was banned in New York City. In 1933, Fiorello Henry La Guardia ran for mayor, promising to rid NYC of corruption and organized crime – an admirable goal for a political candidate. The five-foot nothing man needed a win, so he picked on someone his own size: pinball. La Guardia declared pinball a gambling game; said it was ruled by the mob in a racket to steal lunch money from children. So, he banned it *"for the children."*

It wasn't just a ban – it was a public relations crusade. They put out warrants and police swarmed into bars, bowling alleys and other establishments. "Family fun," as pinball was known to be, was over. *Dozens* of cities followed suit, including Atlanta, New Orleans, Los Angeles, and

Chicago. Ironically, Chicago was not only the birthplace of pinball during the Great Depression but was also the manufacturing hub for some 90% of all pinball machines. The unreasonable law sacrificed thousands of jobs across the nation for decades...all because of the little man with big political aspirations. There was no proof of mob involvement or kids spending lunch money on pinball. It was all a lie, yet many states went along with it. Collusion on this level should *rattle you awake*.

It is clear there are no limits certain people, posing as leaders, will mislead the public for personal gain and fame. These are charlatans; Pied Pipers who have mastered the art of deception. They have duped millions with their influence and carry-on as if they ought to be worshiped for it. We don't need political saviors; we need to empower ourselves to know more, to do better, and discern fact from fiction.

It is time we took off the rose-colored glasses in order to see the red flags.

GQ journalist and pinball wizard, Roger Sharpe, was a reluctant player in this game. He refused multiple requests from the amusement association to rally against the ruling that pinball was a game of chance, and therefore a gambling game. After all, he had a pinball machine in his house, so what did he care? That ridiculous law wasn't affecting his hobby in the least.

And then he had a change of heart.

Agreeing to speak up, he appeared in a NYC court to

demonstrate pinball as a game of strategy, not luck. Upon seeing this demonstration, in 1976, the 35-year ban was instantly lifted.

Mayor La Guardia was long-gone by then, but his name has been memorialized in many ways, including the 1939 opening of La Guardia Airport. It seems this tradition, of heralding shady political figures, lives on. The council member who overturned his law is the one we should be celebrating. A reasonable man of conscience, he could not deny what he saw with his own eyes.

"Pinball: The Man Who Saved the Game," is the true story of Roger Sharpe's obsession with pinball, yet it is so much more: **He turned his passion into action**. The movie, which has won *multiple* awards over the past two years, is cleverly and comically narrated by Sharpe. Life lessons and one-liners are delightfully delivered throughout this must-see film. I've seen it three times, so far. Feel-good movies that end well are always worth a repeat.

Among the many takeaways this movie offers, the main point is this: lies and deception still abound. La Guardia wielded influence over millions of people, nationwide, *for the sake of the children*. Uh-huh, sure. That others in power went along with the sham, may be no surprise, but it should be. What else is being done "for the children"?

How about if we ask this, instead: What is being done *to* the children? Why is it "excess deaths" has risen by 22% in children aged 1 – 14 years old? How has "excess deaths" become a term we use these days? What the hell is going on??

How is it that unelected people and organizations are implementing life-altering laws? Are you aware of the

FDA's recent labelling of pregnancy as an illness? They did it for one reason: emergency use authorization of the abortion pill. That's right: the "morning after pill" has been put back on the market because pregnancy is now considered an illness. If that doesn't make you sick, what will?

What else will they do? Medical dictatorship is real. This extends to the World Health Organization, led by Tedros. Would you trust a stranger to dictate when, how, and what you should put into your body? That's what the Pandemic Treaty is all about: medical dictatorship. If you look into his past, you will discover he was, (as I choose my words carefully): a *really* bad guy to a lot of people in his home country. Seek to know, please look it up.

◆ ◆ ◆

Seeker or Beaker

I am embarrassed at having been a beaker – someone who allowed others to fill my head with their La Guardia-like B.S. I didn't know what I didn't know; didn't know to ask; never thought things were as messed-up as I've learned them to be. At first, cognitive dissonance, mental discomfort that results from holding two conflicting beliefs, values, or attitudes, and not being able to grasp the new knowledge, shook me something fierce. The depth of betrayal at the hands of trusted sources sparked so much doubt and disbelief. Heck, I used to say, "We're all one and it's all good." It made me feel better, sure. However, it wasn't the full picture.

I was guilty of wearing rose-colored glasses caked with a lifetime residue of believing everyone was good, meant well, and wanted to help others. I paid the price for delusional thinking, too. In 2022, I published a book meant to be a field guide to spotting trouble before it becomes your problem. It was written in response to what was discovered as a Seeker: a global clown show on parade. Their behavior inspired the title, "*How to Deal with a Dumbass: what to do and say when they come your way.*" Five red flags, including "Apathy" and "Erratic" are highlighted, as are strategies to break up, break out and break free from the influence of chaos-causing people. Stories of how I blindly trusted the wrong people, a "Repeat Offender" myself, make this a humorous, memoir-esque book.

Indeed, my Polly Anna outlook got me into major hot water, over-and-over again. Becoming the poster child for what not to do also landed me featured guest roles on the Tyra Banks & Steve Harvey talk shows, so I guess that's a win? Admitting I was blind to evil, or ill-intending people, has been embarrassing, but so what? Acknowledge, forgive and move on. **Action alleviates anxiety.** We are a product of our environment until we seek to unlearn and enlighten ourselves.

Speaking of seeking, this just happened and will impact those of you who take to the internet when you need information; health-related information, in particular:

YouTube has recently banned anything related to health that doesn't align with the General Medical consensus. In other words, *if any information related to health doesn't agree with the World Health Organization*, they won't necessarily always take down the video but they're going to change the algorithms; they're going to replace those videos that were popular, ones that had lots of likes and lots of engagement with medical information.

This new partnership with YouTube is supposed to protect you against misinformation and promote high quality health information. However, their definition of misinformation is biased.

Dr. Eric Berg, D.C., is the go-to guy for millions of people on social media. He has offered natural options to those who did not want, or had little success, with traditional medicines. With 7,607 testimonials and success stories on his website, it is clear he is helping in a big way. He received that alarming message from YouTube, recently.

"Some of my biggest health topics have been silenced. Although it may be a sign I'm doing something right, it blocks the potential of millions from being educated on natural health alternatives I've spent years developing." -Dr Berg (pictured here)

Seeing censorship in motion raises my ire. A small example: Dr. Berg always ranked first in "keto diet" searches. Mayo Clinic now tops the list. They are not in favor of keto and apparently want you to think the same way. Now, you must dig deeper; become a Seeker. His website is: **https://www.drberg.com/**

In a previous chapter, **"This Bugs Me,"** I pointed you to a video showing an easy method for discerning good food from not-so-hot or good for you. The technique, known as muscle testing, utilizes the body's innate wisdom for discernment. Yesterday, I discovered that channel has been removed.

Coincidence? The recently-held World Economic Forum's focus was on "misinformation." A revealing display of power was stated as "We pretty much own the media, the papers, and broadcasting. We get to decide what is put out there and we need to control the spread of misinformation." Hmmm. Once again, unelected people are interfering with our lives. There is no consent on our part, just rulings dictating access to information, and companies like YouTube taking action in lockstep with these people. Elected officials, just like the ones who made pinball illegal, are clearly complicit. The 'go along to get along' approach doesn't maintain freedoms we are all quietly losing in big ways.

◆ ◆ ◆

Have you heard the words "turbo cancer"? This was not in use until recently, like "excess deaths." Perhaps your news sources failed to mention a recent 400% increase in cancer; how people are being diagnosed with stage four cancer in a matter of months after following the advice of "leaders" to medically 'protect' themselves and their children. The inference here should be obvious…and *it should rattle the crap out of you.*

My father suffered from melanoma. Hundreds of stitches across his forehead stood as proof of an ongoing and ineffective course of treatment, mandated by men in white lab coats. Tumors were removed from within 2 millimeters of his brain. Every three months, hundreds of lesions were 'burned' off his face, neck and arms. Can you imagine the pain?

One day, he ran into a Native American Indian who recommended Essiac tea. He said the 8-herb formula would not interfere with any medications or treatments. It has been used "forever" by the Ojibwa Indians with great results. Made popular by Nurse Caisse, a Canadiaan cancer nurse, Essiac is her name spelled backwards. She went through hell-and-high water fighting the V=government to allow its use. My dad picked-up a retail store version, Flor-Essence, and informed his doctor about adding it to his diet.

The dermatologist laughed, "There, there, Don, you will always be my patient." That was the last he ever saw of my father. Essiac worked. Considering my father's lifelong battle with melanoma, the blessing cannot be overstated. *Thank you, Nurse Caisse.*

Excitedly, I did research and lo & behold, found a direct link to genuine Essiac (be aware, there are imposters), at a huge savings. Instead of the expensive, pre-mixed variety, you steep the powder at home. It's simple to do, doesn't have a bad taste and won't interfere with current medical 'routines.' In fact, it is reported to flush out die-off from chemo treatments. These are not medical claims, just anecdotal feedback from my contact at Discount Essiac Tea, Linda Paulhus. Since her passing, son, Bryan, and his wife, Gina, maintain the business, growing organic herbs for their stellar product.

I went on the warpath, appearing on talk shows, writing press releases, and selling my "special report" in newspapers across the country. I got some support, but absolutely *zero* came from the cancer-related associations and oncologists. It was so frustrating! Little did I know at the time that JD Rockefeller not only created highly-addictive petroleum-based medications, but when evidence proved they were causing cancer, he then founded the American Cancer Society in response.

> Problem. Reaction. Solution.

Doctors, (a word ironically close to "indoctrinated"), were arrested and lost their license to practice medicine. You see, Rockefeller also changed the medical texts, removing and forbidding any mention of natural remedies. And now, they are being censored, just as I was yesterday when YouTube removed my comments telling a gal about Essiac. This is happening.

> *Condemnation without investigation*
> *is the height of ignorance*

I lost count how many times I heard, "If my doctor doesn't know about it, it must not be real/legit." After three years, I stopped trying to reach those who most needed this information. It was exhausting. But I never stopped recommending Essiac and the Paulhus family. Take a look at why:

Shanion Hart
Yes! I love this tea and I always drink. It has taken sun spots off my face. Spots I've had for years. It cured a bad lock jaw for me. It calms my anxiety and it has cured an ingrown toenail issue I've had all my life. My husband has vitiligo and it has brought some of his pigmentation back. This has taken a bit longer, but it is slowly working for him. I hope this helps you. Best wishes! ☺

One man's wife suffered from horrible gum disease. Her periodontist fell off his swivel chair when, two months into using Essiac, her gums never looked so healthy.

https://www.discount-essiac-tea.com/essiac-testimonials.html
(Click on the links to jump directly to a specific condition, or scroll down to see all of the Essiac testimonials.)

The product is very affordable! Save even more using this coupon code: ALEXIS10

It isn't a gift unless the receiver wants it.

Case in point:

My father's wife, who witnessed his recovery from melanoma, refused the Essiac I gave her. She preferred to treat her stage four breast cancer the good ol' fashioned way. When I asked her oncologist 'what if?' and 'what's next?' questions, he said, "You better wait outside." Yeah, I get it. The indoctrinated leading the indoctrinated leaves little room for inquiry.

When did white lab coats become the sign of an all-knowing savior? His response said it all; so did hers.

I have been certified as a Chiropractic Assistant by the Palmer College of Chiropractic, and worked in the field for decades. I have seen what the body can do if it is given the right herbs and treatments. I have also witnessed what the medical system has done to my family as well as thousands of strangers' lives.

Ask why before you comply. Please question the narrative and those who are pushing it, especially when it is couched as "for the children." "Turbo cancer" and "excess deaths" should not be in our vocabulary.

We can no longer hope the ship will right itself as it has in the past. No one has our backs and 'hope' is not a strategy. This is far from hopeless, though. In fact, now that you know better you can do better.

> *"In order to change something, we must first become aware that it can be changed. If you are unaware that something can be changed then perhaps you are dependent on some other intervention; passive rather than proactive."* -Alan Chapman, Rattled Awake: Volume Seven

How about if we look at what *is* happening and take back authority over our lives? *Seekers* look and love to learn.

Start by looking beyond mainstream media for one's daily diet of "news." Their scripted broadcasts are not telling you everything, by design. If you only hear half the truth, what is the other half?

Try out this YouTube channel, "**Redacted**" for a week or two. The host/couple both come from major news networks and reporting backgrounds. Their broadcasts are current, diverse and relevant. You will hear things 'lamestream' media do not share.

> Hang on! Public Schools are now PAYING kids to Indoctrinate Them? | Redacted w Natali Morris

As one YouTube commenter put said: If the cause was legitimate it wouldn't need to bribe people to promote it.

It's all happening. Do you see it? Ignorance is bliss, until it isn't.

◆ ◆ ◆

Thirty-plus years after a false case was built to create La Guardia's political career, a pinball wizard came along to set the record straight once-and-for-all. Roger Sharpe's choice to question the established law, and the establishment behind it, was all it took to take down a massive house of cards. Once he got past his own little world, his personal bubble of content, and saw the bigger picture, he became the stand-up guy who changed history.

You, too, can be the person that changes lives for the better. Take action in your home, at the grocery store, in your kid's lives. Please start to notice where your freedoms are being whittled away. Use your voice. Post and share your insights. Give a video a thumb's up. "They" already have your viewing history, so why not show support for the efforts being made by the host or post? Lead the way as a Seeker and sovereign-minded person would. The future needs us all to stand up and stand our ground *today.*

When it comes to making a choice, seek outside the traditional sources. Ask for a sign, and trust your inner GPS to guide you. It's the only way to go: inward, before you move forward. That insatiable curiosity you were born with is just waiting for you to seek it out, once again.

It's pretty cut-and-dried:

Are you a Seeker, or a Beaker, waiting to be told what to think, eat, be and do? The choice is always yours.

Sounds like a red pill/blue pill moment, doesn't it?

"The Matrix wasn't just a film; it was a documentary."

– Sophia Stewart, the real writer and creator of "The Matrix"

For What It's Worth - worth a listen again because we do need to look at what's going down.

Lonnee Rey, ghost writer, book producer and 11x author, also conducts transformational writing workshops then publishes writers' heartfelt messages a few days later in the best-selling "**Rattled Awake**" series.

Winner, *Best Indie Book of the Year, 2023*. "LGBTQ+ ABCs for Grown-Ups" Lonnee Rey, Editor

"**How to Deal with a Dumbass: what to do and say when they come your way**," is credited with helping a mature reader escape a dangerous cult in Norway, while helping others navigate their way to making friends better. Amazon also carries "**Life lessons learned from a lousy mother**." Written and published in five days, this 20-minute read is a comfort for those who did not have June Cleaver for a mother, either.

Lonnee is on a mission to bring awareness to alarming trends regarding our food supply.

Listen to these important alerts where she has voiced all chapters: **YouTube**.

Over 60 short episodes, based on her "Dumbass" book, can be found here: **https:// podcasters.spotify.com/ pod/show/ howtodealwithadumbass**

THE RATTLED TATTLER NEWS

The Rattled Tattler

BREAKING NEWS

DON'T LOOK NOW   VOL. SEVEN

GREEN ENERGY GIVEN PERMISSION TO ABOLISH THOUSANDS OF DOLPHINS WITH SOUND WAVES. For the record, French- and Dutch-owned Atlantic Shores and Danish-owned Ørsted asked permission to hurt whales, dolphins, porpoises, and seals. And they got it.

Associated Press Gets It Wrong: Wind Farm Contractors Acknowledge Turbines Harm Dolphins, Whales
Diana Furchtgott-Roth / December 28, 2023

Members of the Northwest Atlantic Marine Alliance practice a necropsy on the carcass of a humpback whale at Lido Beach in Long Island, New York, on Jan. 31, 2024.

The male humpback washed up on the shore of Long Island the day before. (Photo: Kena Betancur/AFP/Getty Images)

SPECIAL EDITION

DON'T LOOK NOW   VOL. SIX

MMPA Regulatory Definitions (50 CFR 216.3):
Level A Harassment: Harassment refers to actions that pose potential harm or discomfort for marine mammals in their native environments, including pursuit, torture, or irritation.

The law is specific, yet, permission was granted to do harm. How do you put your name on a doc like that? Who are you people?

If they needed permission, then the danger was already known. Who got paid to allow "excess deaths" to go down? They are all knowing accomplices in this crime, but using frequency to un-alive thousands of these beautiful creatures in the name of green energy? Greed energy is more like it.

It doesn't matter NOW that the overseas green energy corporations have pulled-out of the project. Who shall be held accountable, a faceless corporate logo? If a 'person' did that, do you think it would fly?

Secondly, perhaps we need to look at "green energy" with more scrutiny? The cost seems really unfriendly to the environment, doesn't it? Can you imagine being killed by sound waves?? Dolphins, with their hypersensitivity, must have been screaming underwater.

Frequency warfare is abominable. Look up "Havana Syndrome" sometime. Yikes. Those poor people...American people, to be precise.

Why does this, or Havana Syndrome matter to you? Because the clowns on parade are getting away with murder. What else will they do if no one's looking?

Truth should not fear investigation. Question the narrative, glossy packaging and nice-sounding names. Are you a Seeker or Beaker?

    One person can make a difference, and every person should try. -JFK, Jr.

These are my views, and do not represent the opinions of others in this publication.

Until next time, I am the Rattled Tattler,

Lonnee Rey, ED., "Rattled Awake" Anthologies

AN OPEN INVITATION

The Rattled Awake 'movement' is an ongoing series dedicated to promoting messages from everyday people on a mission to share their legacy messages in print, forever.

Writing workshops continue to inspire both first-time writers as well as experienced writers - all of whom benefit from the collaboration as well as the training.

If you have ever wanted live coaching and help getting your thoughts down on paper, then out into the world, this is your chance.

"Don't die with the music still in you." Dr. Wayne Dyer

Write one chapter - in one weekend - and one week later, enjoy the status "Co-author of the Best Seller, Rattled Awake" forever.

Visit OfficialRattledAwake.com

for more information about the next workshop.

RATTLED AWAKE

RATTLED AWAKE: VOLUME ONE

Over the past 5 years, what is the single biggest event that caused you to completely change your perspective?

What you are about to read are "shook" moments that completely changed the writer's perspectives about themselves, and life, given the impact of dramatic, and unexpected shifts each of us have experienced in these unprecedented times of great change.

Rattled Awake: Volume One

Written together in a single weekend, these authors bring you their legacy messages and truly RATTLED AWAKE moments:

You're never too old to rewrite your next chapter and change up your script ~Chef Jill Sullivan
Still So Much Life to Live ~Chris Freer
Not a "Cougar" or a "Karen" and Worth WAY More than 9 Pence… ~Erika Warfield
Transfer your Setbacks into Remarkable Comebacks. ~LeeAnna Stock-Luoma
Look Beyond the Box, For We Are So Much More ~Susannah Dawn.

Beneath the Perfect Score: The Silent Crisis of Student Suicides in Asian Cultures ~Dr. Constance Leyland
The Bipolar Pen: Unleashing the Gift of a Writer ~Nicole Angai-Galindo
Live Your Purpose Now! ~Russ Hedge
Growing With The Flow..~Willie J.
The Pressure Cooker ~Lonnee Rey
It's All an Illusion. ~Steve Kidd

Are you ready to be Rattled Awake?

Rattled Awake: Volume Two

No matter what has happened over the past five years, allow optimism enter. Each "Rattled Awake" moment can bring you a gift. Enjoy the treasures each author shares so freely here, and let them inspire you to rewrite your next chapter.

Lesley Mouton...That Ain't No Genie in a Bottle!
Bob Witty...This Has to Stop: A True Story About Veteran Suicide
Jill Sullivan...Caretaking for Grandma Joan, "The Candy Lady"
Doug Thompson... The Universe's Storyteller
Brian Schulman... You Are the Light in the Basement
Nancy Debra Barrows... Becoming
Gene Petrino... From Apathy to Action: Unleashing the Warrior Within
Michaela Riordan Turner, PsyD... Daddy Rocks!
Chiyedza Nyahuye... Miracles on the Playground
Willie J.... Surviving to Thrive
Niki Bell...Mastering Mysticism and Prevailing!

Lonnee Rey... This Bugs Me

Rattled Awake: Volume Three

Over the last 5 years, what single event rattled you awake? We have all been through a lot, especially in the last five years. What shook you?

These eight authors have eight uncommon experiences to share as they show you what it was like to pivot, improve and prevail. All of them shifted with the changing tides, becoming better, not bitter, and bring you nuggets of wisdom mined from the depths of their souls. enJOY!

Dare to Surrender...Lisa Marree
She's All HeArt...Michelle Laaks
Rising from Within...Dr. Nhu Truong
Grow Through...Wendy Wiseman
Laugh, Play, Heal...Chiyedza Nyahuye
Phoenix Awakening...Crystal Behe
Gremlins...Kim Groshek
Bend, Don't Break...George Monty
The Art of Traveling Light...Lonnee Rey

Rattled Awake: Volume Four

"Over the past 5 years, what is the single biggest event that caused you to completely change your perspective for the better?"

We have all been impacted by dramatic shifts in life as we knew it to be. Who have we become as a result of these events?

These authors share one response in common: they became better, not bitter. Driven to share their legacy message of hope and inspiration with you, they gathered together over one weekend to write their hearts out - to leave you feeling uplifted, perhaps a bit introspective and motivated to move beyond self-limiting concepts.

The FOURTH in a series, Rattled Awake is proud to present these life-changing stories of how one incident dramatically shifted each of these authors lives' for the better:
Doma Nunzio...Find the Others
Brian Luoma...Quite the Fish Tail
Tonya Davis...Letting Go to Grow
Wendy Wiseman...Slow Your Roll
Dr. Michaela Turner...I Solve a Problem
Lonnee Rey...Untying the Knots

Rattled Awake: Volume Five

We have all been impacted by dramatic shifts in life as we knew it to be. Who have we become as a result of these events?

No moss is growing under their feet.

These authors share one response in common: they became better, not bitter. Driven to share their legacy message of hope and inspiration with you, they gathered together over one weekend to write their hearts out - to leave you motivated and moving in the right direction.
Are you ready to be Rattled Awake?

Shaken From the Darkness...Robb Profancik
I never wanted to be a mother...Lisa Marree
Break A Leg...Wendy Wiseman
Peace of Mind...Lonnee Rey
Are you sure?...Mario Bekes
Cracks in the Foundation...Chef Shawn Monroe
NO Regrets...Michelle Laaks Rattled Awake An Open Invitation

Rattled Awake:: The Podcasters' Edition

We have all been impacted by dramatic shifts in life as we knew it to be. Who have we become as a result of these events? Answers vary but the Universal messages are timeless.

Rattled Awake, Volume Six, The Podcasters' Edition, is blessed to have these podcasters join the movement.

People who podcast are a unique type - the type you want to know - and in this edition are INCREDIBLE stories which peel-and-reveal sides you don't normally get to see from podcasters.

Mark O'Brien - The Anxious Voyage
Michael Fritzius - Running, For Life
Zen Benefiel - Silver Linings
Sam Liebowitz - My Psychedelic Rattle
Joi Brooks - Serendipity
Mark Reid - No Obligation To Stay The Same
Kat Polsinelli - The Silent Storm
Lonnee Rey - Return to Sender
What shook you recently? Their answers may surprise you.

Printed in Great Britain
by Amazon